ORANGES Evaluation Final Report

For the US DOT sponsored Evaluation of the ORANGES Electronic Payment Systems Field Operational Test

US DOT/Volpe National Transportation Systems Center

December 6, 2004

Foreword

This document is the US DOT evaluation final report for the ORANGES field operational test, which was conducted from August 2003 through July 2004.

Table of Contents

Appendix A – Test Plans
Appendix B – Discussion Group Pre-Screening, Scripts and Notes Summaries
Appendix C – Minutes from the Evaluation Team Meetings and Conference Calls

Executive Summary

Background

In 2000, the US DOT awarded an FOT grant to a multimodal consortium of transportation agencies in the Orlando region. The summary of the original US DOT Request For Proposals[1] is as follows:

- "The U.S. Department of Transportation (US DOT) announces a Request for Proposals from eligible applicants for an operational test of an electronic payment system for transit fare collection, parking payment, electronic toll collection and other applications. The US DOT is interested in identifying and evaluating issues associated with the establishment of partnerships between public transit service providers and other entities in the development and use of multiple-application electronic payment systems. The Department is specifically interested in an operational test of a payment system that includes a variety of applications, but must at a minimum include transit fare collection, parking payment and electronic toll collection."

The RFP also informed proposers that a separately funded evaluation of the project would be undertaken by a third party contractor, and that the participating agencies would be required to participate in and support the evaluation effort.

The ORANGES partnership involved both public and private sector participants:

- **Public Sector Partners:** The Central Florida Regional Transportation Authority (doing business as LYNX), the Orlando-Orange County Expressway Authority (OOCEA) and the City of Orlando Parking Bureau were the Public Agency Partners, with LYNX also serving as the Federal grantee and manager of the FOT.

- **Private Sector Partners:** Private sector firms implemented the FOT system under contract, on behalf of the Public Partners. Post Buckley Schuh & Jernigan (PBS&J) was contracted to LYNX as their General ITS & APTS Consultant, with FOT responsibilities including program management, oversight and implementation support. TranSend[2] was the Lead Technical Partner responsible for system development and

---

[1] This was originally released in 1999 as the "Request for Proposals for an Operational Test of an Electronic Payment System for Transportation and Other Applications", building on an earlier "Request for Letters of Interest to Participate in an Operational Test of an Electronic Payment System for Transit Fare Collection and Other Applications" released in 1998.

[2] During the demonstration, Touch Technology International was reorganized, and the part of the original organization responsible for supporting the demonstration became known as TranSend.

integration, implementing and operating the clearinghouse – contracted to LYNX. Additional services and equipment suppliers included Ascom Transport Systems (transit smart card validators), EFKON (toll plaza readers and smart card accepting transponder equipment), Gemplus (dual interface smart cards) and McGann Parking Systems (parking garage readers). Ascom, EFKON and McGann provided equipment, as well as some installation, configuration and integration effort, at free or reduced cost to assist the goals of the FOT.

The FOT implemented a central payment and clearinghouse system using core technology from TranSend. Payment transactions completed at smart card readers operated by individual agencies were transmitted to the ORANGES clearinghouse for settlement to agency-owned revenue accounts.

The scope of the FOT involved a limited scale test demonstration under revenue service conditions:

- **Card base:** A single card could be loaded with multiple payment applications, thus allowing the card to be accepted for payment across all agencies. The agencies intended to maintain 800-1200 smart cards in active use at all times during the test. However, during the demonstration, the active card base[3] remained below 160.

- **Transit component:** LYNX equipped two (2) routes; Links 13 and 15. Each of these routes connected post-secondary educational institutions with the downtown area.

- **Toll component:** The Orlando-Orange County Expressway Authority (OOCEA) equipped selected lanes of the Holland East toll plaza on State Route 408 to accept the EFKON transponder with a smart card, as well as installed "Touch and Go" smart card accepting validators in selected manual lanes, for each direction. Smart card acceptance through transponders in five lanes (two in each direction plus one reversible lane) was deferred one or two months from the FOT launch. The Holland East plaza is a 14-lane facility. Lanes 1-7 operate westbound, lanes 9-14 operate eastbound, and lane 8 is reversible. This plaza accounts for approximately 20% of the revenue and transactions annually for OOCEA.

- **Parking component:** The City of Orlando Parking Bureau equipped cashier booths in the Central Boulevard, Library and Market Street garages.

- **Revaluing facilities:** Each agency offered facilities for smart card issuance and revaluing. This included points of sale at agency-operated customer service facilities,

---

[3] A card became classified as active once first used, but subsequently classified as inactive if not used for three consecutive weeks.

selected attended toll lanes and parking garage exits, and some locations operated by third parties (additional details on revaluing locations and payment methods accepted are provided below). Transit passes continued to be sold only through LYNX facilities and transponders continued to be available only through OOCEA facilities.

The system test configuration strategy was specifically designed to isolate the smart card payment system from the existing legacy systems where necessary in the operation at each agency. This strategy offered the least risk to existing operations and revenue management.

Evaluation Goals/Measures and Test Hypotheses

Tables ES-1 and ES-2 identify the set of quantitative and qualitative goals and measures initially established for the evaluation, developed through the consensus-building process. The tables also list the fundamental test hypothesis for each quantitative goal and measure. This initial consensus created the basis to develop test plans and investigate sources for the baseline data collection effort.

Joint Account Use

As mentioned above, the agencies had adopted a target of maintaining 800-1200 active cards throughout the demonstration period. Figure ES-1 summarizes the cumulative number of cards issued by the agencies over the course of the analysis period. From the start of card issuance in August 2003 through late January 2004, over 1000 cards had been issued – and roughly 200 more cards were issued through June 2004. However, the percentage of active cards (as shown in Figure ES-2) remained at roughly 10% through June 2004, and subsequently gradually decreased to roughly 6% over the final month or so of the demonstration. This placed the number of active cards below 160 throughout the trial, which was well below the target.

The decline in card use towards the end of the demonstration can be reasonably attributed, to some degree, to the fact that cardholders were reminded around this time that the demonstration was coming to an end after July 2004, as well as to a normal summer decline in commuting activity.

Figure ES-1. Cumulative Cards Issued

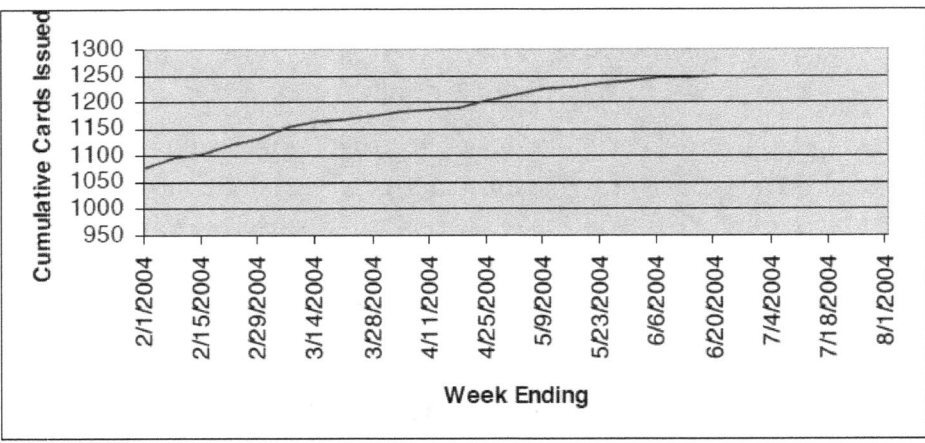

Figure ES-2. Percentage Active Cards

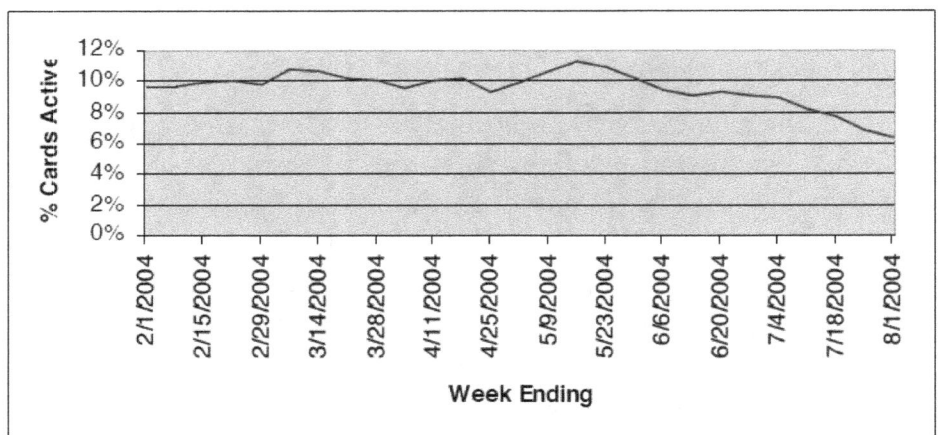

The most common modal pattern of weekly card use was single mode use for parking, followed by single mode use for tolls. Over the course of the demonstration, multimodal card use for parking and tolls somewhat increased, but there was virtually no multimodal card use involving transit.

The evolution of the average card stored value balance over the February 2004 through July 2004 period is summarized in Figure ES-3. The trend was for the average stored value to decline over the duration of the trial. In fact, if this graph is compared with the percentage active cards graph in Figure ES-2, the shape is very similar. This suggests that the primary reason for the down wards shift in the average stored value balance was an increasing number of inactive cards carrying a small residual balance.

Figure ES-3. Average Stored Value Balance

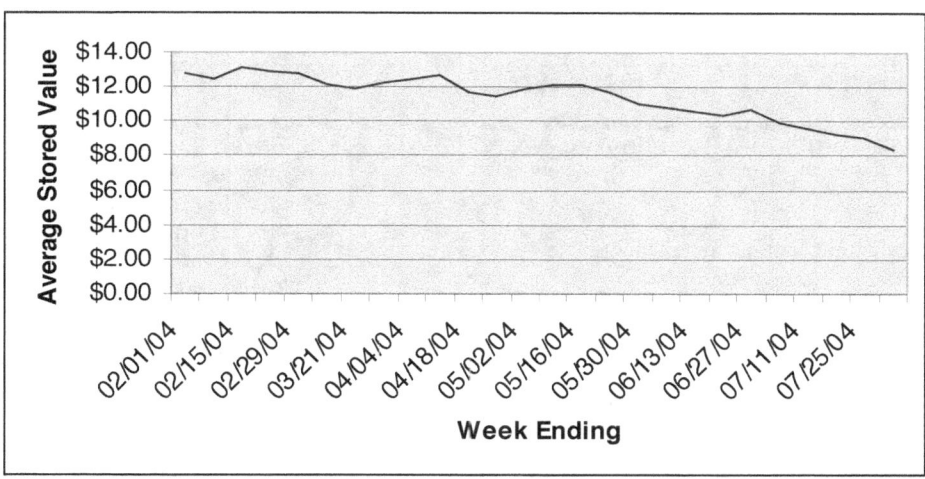

Before and After Comparisons

This section compares the statistical analysis results for quantitative goals for which there was both before and after testing. In addition, this section presents conclusions based on these comparisons that seem reasonable.

Note that, where the 95% confidence intervals for the before and after data do not overlap, this is interpreted as providing evidence supporting a statistically significant change. Where the confidence intervals do overlap, larger samples might have resulted in evidence supporting a statistically significant change (i.e., through establishing narrower confidence intervals that eliminate the overlap).

Quantitative Goal 4 – Reduce Transaction Times

Parking

The before testing statistical analysis concluded:

- Three garages combined: At the 95% confidence level, the average transaction time was expected to be 23.3 s +/- 5% (i.e., between 22.1 and 24.5 seconds, 95% of the time).

The after testing statistical analysis concluded:

- Three garages combined: At the 95% confidence level, the average transaction time was expected to be 19.9 s +/- 6% (i.e., between 18.7 and 21.1 seconds, 95% of the time).

Table ES-1: Quantitative Evaluation Goals/Measures and Test Hypotheses

FOT Evaluation Goal	Measure	Test Hypothesis
1. Increase parking revenue	• Revenue received	• Revenue will increase from parking payment equipment that accepts smart cards, due to increased equipment availability and improved customer convenience. The degree of revenue increase will vary for different types of parking equipment.
2. Increase transponder market penetration	• Number of smart card users that newly acquire a transponder	• Of the smart card users, some will choose to newly acquire a transponder
3. Reduce transaction times	• Average transaction times	• Smart card transactions will be quicker than cash payment, so average time will reduce if there is a shift from cash to smart card.
4. Increase prepaid revenue share	• % revenue prepaid	• The % of revenue that is prepaid will increase for equipment that accepts smart cards
5. Reduce monthly pass distribution costs	• Procurement, inventory, delivery, commissions for any conventional passes made available on smart cards	• The number of conventional passes being distributed will decrease, thus reducing distribution costs
6. Increase automated payment equipment uptime	• % equipment availability	• The decreased use of cash will improve equipment reliability
7. Cardholders use the joint account[4]	• Card use profiles • Average prepaid balance • Modal use profile	• Customers that activate joint transportation accounts will maintain a prepaid balance and use the card frequently. Multimodal use by individual cardholders will most often involve tolls and parking.

---

[4] The joint account involved the ability to use one or more different types of smart card with smart card readers installed at transit, parking and toll facilities. The joint account did not involve use of the same account for both smart cards and toll transponders.

Table ES-2: Qualitative Goals/Measures and Test Hypotheses

FOT Evaluation Goal	Measure
8. Understand customer perceptions • **General benefits** • **Ease of use** • **Convenience of revaluing**	• Customer feedback
9. Understand operations/maintenance staff perceptions, including: • **General benefits** • **Reduced payment disputes** • **Reduced transfer abuse** • **Ease of customer use** • **Maintenance**	• Operations/maintenance staff feedback
10. Understand planning/management staff perceptions, including: • **General benefits** • **More comprehensive data collection**	• Planning/management staff feedback
11. Understand interagency perceptions, including: • **General institutional issues** • **Interagency collaboration**	• Partnership feedback

Comparing the two analyses provides evidence supporting a statistically significant reduction in the average transaction time. This supports the test hypothesis that the conversion of some of the cash transactions to ORANGES would reduce the average transaction time by reducing the duration of these transactions.

As discussed in Goal 5, a drop in the use of monthly permits between the before and after periods resulted in the after period having a greater cash share. This strengthens the significance of the reduced average transaction time, since the expected effect would have been an increase in average transaction time.

Transit

The before testing statistical analysis concluded:

• Link 13: At the 95% confidence level, the average transaction time was expected to be 13.0 s +/- 4% (i.e., between 12.5 and 13.5 seconds, 95% of the time).

• Link 15: At the 95% confidence level, the average transaction time was expected to be 10.6 s +/- 3% (i.e., between 10.3 and 10.9 seconds, 95% of the time).

The after testing statistical analysis concluded:

- Link 15: At the 95% confidence level, the average transaction time was expected to be 9.5 s +/- 6% (i.e., between 8.9 and 10.1 seconds, 95% of the time).

A before and after comparison was undertaken only for Link 15, as a result of the limited availability of after data due to LYNX APC equipment failures. With less data in the Link 15 after sample than the Link 15 before sample, the Link 15 after data confidence interval is substantially wider than the Link 15 before data confidence interval. Nonetheless, comparing the two Link 15 analyses provides evidence supporting a statistically significant reduction in the average transaction time. This supports the test hypothesis that the conversion of some of the cash transactions to ORANGES would reduce the average transaction time by reducing the duration of these transactions.

As discussed under Goal 5, however, there were few ORANGES transactions, as well as an overall shift from cash to period passes, between the before and after data. This suggests that the observed reduction in average transaction time is likely more attributable to the increased pass use than to the ORANGES transactions.

Quantitative Goal 5 – Increase Prepaid Revenue Share

Parking

The before testing statistical analysis concluded:

- Central Boulevard Garage: At the 95% confidence level, the average prepaid revenue share was expected to be 52% +/- 12% (i.e., between 45% and 58%, 95% of the time).

- Library Garage: At the 95% confidence level, the average prepaid revenue share was expected to be 46% +/- 16% (i.e., between 39% and 53%, 95% of the time).

- Market Garage: At the 95% confidence level, the average prepaid revenue share was expected to be 47% +/- 14% (i.e., between 40% and 54%, 95% of the time).

The after testing statistical analysis concluded:

- Central Boulevard Garage: At the 95% confidence level, the average prepaid revenue share was expected to be 45% +/- 13% (i.e., between 39% and 51%, 95% of the time).

- Library Garage: At the 95% confidence level, the average prepaid revenue share was expected to be 38% +/- 8% (i.e., between 35% and 41%, 95% of the time).

- Market Garage: At the 95% confidence level, the average prepaid revenue share was expected to be 33% +/- 10% (i.e., between 30% and 37%, 95% of the time).

Comparing the two analyses for each of the garages does not provide evidence supporting a statistically significant change in the prepaid revenue share for the Central and Library garages, but does provide evidence supporting a statistically significant decrease in the prepaid revenue share for the Market garage.

The before data spans the October 2002 through March 2003 time period, and the after data spans the June 2004 through August 2004 time period. The before and after data indicate a drop in both overall and monthly permit parking revenue during the summer after period, which may result from reduced parking use by commuters (who are most likely to use a monthly permit) during summer vacation periods.

Given the longer transaction times for cash relative to prepaid transactions, the observed similar or higher share for cash transactions in the after period, all things being equal, should have tended to increase the average parking transaction time. This serves to strengthen the importance of the observed decrease in average parking transaction time under Goal 4, suggesting an even greater reduced transaction time effect for the ORANGES card transactions.

Transit

The before testing statistical analysis concluded:

- Link 13: At the 95% confidence level, the average prepaid ridership share was expected to be 58% +/- 3% (i.e., between 57% and 60%, 95% of the time).

- Link 15: At the 95% confidence level, the average prepaid ridership share was expected to be 57% +/- 2% (i.e., between 56% and 58%, 95% of the time).

The after testing statistical analysis concluded:

- Link 13: At the 95% confidence level, the average prepaid ridership share was expected to be 67% +/- 1% (i.e., between 66% and 67%, 95% of the time).

- Link 15: At the 95% confidence level, the average prepaid ridership share was expected to be 62% +/- 2% (i.e., between 61% and 64%, 95% of the time).

Comparing the two analyses for each of the routes provides evidence supporting a statistically significant increase in the prepaid ridership share. Examining the before and after data reveals that there were few ORANGES transactions, but a clear shift from cash to prepaid passes between the two time periods. This suggests that the reduced average transaction time discussed under Goal 4 is likely more attributable to the increase in pass use than to the ORANGES transactions.

Quantitative Goal 6 – Increase Automated Payment Equipment Uptime

Tolls

The before testing statistical analysis concluded:

- At the 95% confidence level, the average ACM % availability was expected to be 99.38% +/- 0.37% (i.e., between 99.02% and 99.74%, 95% of the time).

The after testing statistical analysis concluded:

- At the 95% confidence level, the average ACM % availability was expected to be 99.82% +/- 0.04% (i.e., between 99.78% and 99.85%, 95% of the time).

Comparing the two analyses provides evidence supporting a statistically significant increase in the ACM % availability. This supports the test hypothesis that introducing the ORANGES transactions reduced the usage of the ACM equipment by reducing the number of cash transactions. Since none of the ORANGES cardholders were previously EPASS transponder users, the ORANGES transactions were expected to have been diverted from former cash transactions.

Transit

The before testing statistical analysis concluded:

- At the 95% confidence level, the average farebox % availability was expected to be 99.12% +/- 0.19% (i.e., between 98.93% and 99.31%, 95% of the time).

The after testing statistical analysis concluded:

- At the 95% confidence level, the average farebox % availability was expected to be 99.30% +/- 0.40% (i.e., between 98.90% and 99.70%, 95% of the time).

Comparing the two analyses does not provide evidence supporting a statistically significant change in the average farebox % availability. For Goal 5, it was concluded that there was an increase in the prepaid revenue share (attributable primarily to a shift from cash to period passes), which, all things being equal, would have been expected to improve the farebox % availability by decreasing the number of cash transactions.

Recommendations for Future Regional Deployments of Multimodal Electronic Payment Systems

Based on the issues and lessons learned from the ORANGES FOT demonstration, the following actions are recommended for agencies intending to deploy a similar multimodal system:

- **Deploy to Fully Meet Traveler Needs:** It appears that one factor limiting card usage in the ORANGES demonstration was that the limited scale of the test configuration did not fully meet traveler needs. LYNX cardholders still needed to use conventional paper transfers and period passes for trips involving non-equipped routes. OOCEA toll users still needed to use a conventional EPASS transponder or cash for non-equipped toll plazas along their travel route. On the other hand, card use at a parking garage addressed the entire payment need for that trip, which may help explain the higher observed usage levels for parking.

- **Foster Institutional Collaboration:** Agencies participating in the ORANGES demonstration established successful technical and interagency operations with a multimodal electronic payment system. This significant and groundbreaking achievement largely resulted from extensive and ongoing institutional collaboration efforts. Project champions took the initiative for ongoing outreach, which helped maintain support from senior management and foster the required new interagency working relationships.

- **Provide Extensive Training:** ORANGES discussion groups indicated that front-line staff involved with card acceptance and revaluing, as well as with customer service, need extensive and ongoing training to be able to operate the system effectively and maintain cardholder confidence.

- **Use Risk Analysis:** Risk analysis can help identify and address risks prior to deployment. The ORANGES demonstration risk analysis identified in advance risks from the limited number of intended cards and acceptance/revaluing locations. Although financial constraints prevented the agencies from increasing the number of acceptance/revaluing locations, the number of issued cards was increased. In the end, this served to help compensate for the low card usage.

- **Ensure Long Term Smart Card Supply:** After placing the initial order, the ORANGES agencies attempted to order additional smart cards but were informed that this card had been discontinued. This illustrates that the future supply of any particular smart card cannot be assured, so it is critical to select smart card readers that can read cards from multiple vendors (or be adapted to do so).

- **Plan on Development Time for Integration Issues with Legacy Equipment:** Parking needed to integrate the card readers with its existing equipment, and integration timing/funding challenges led to excluding parking kiosks and meters from the demonstration. For OOCEA, EFKON equipment – separate from the existing equipment -- was selected to minimize any impact on existing toll plaza systems. However, the smart card reader type supported by this toll equipment was not yet supported by the LYNX fareboxes; this led to LYNX using a stand-alone smart card reader. The point is that significant time was needed to identify and address the various compatibility issues involved with accepting a universal smart card type in the legacy equipment environment of multiple agencies.

- **Monitor System Data During Initial Operations:** Analysis of after data revealed that the system was not handling negative balances correctly. No part of the overall system had been configured with the necessary logic to complete such transactions correctly or to detect/report if such transactions were completed incorrectly. Although this issue was not detected during system acceptance testing, it could have been identified through ongoing periodic reviews of system data by the implementing agencies.

1 Introduction

This report describes the findings of the US DOT-sponsored evaluation of the Orlando (Florida) ORANGES multi-modal Field Operational Test (FOT); the report includes:

- a background description of the ORANGES FOT;

- the Evaluation Strategy and Plan, which established the evaluation goals, measures and test hypotheses;

- the detailed before and after Test Plans, which developed the specific data collection and analysis procedures for each measure and test hypothesis;

- the process used for conducting the before and after discussion group components of the Test Plans;

- the findings from the before and after discussion groups;

- the statistical analysis of the results from the quantitative data collection; and

- a discussion of lessons learned from the ORANGES FOT evaluation.

2 Background Description of the ORANGES Field Operational Test System

In 2000, the US DOT awarded an FOT grant to a multimodal consortium of transportation agencies in the Orlando region. The summary of the original US DOT Request For Proposals[5] is as follows:

- "The U.S. Department of Transportation (US DOT) announces a Request for Proposals from eligible applicants for an operational test of an electronic payment system for transit fare collection, parking payment, electronic toll collection and other applications. The US DOT is interested in identifying and evaluating issues associated with the establishment of partnerships between public transit service providers and other entities in the development and use of multiple-application electronic payment systems. The Department is specifically interested in an operational test of a payment system that includes a variety of applications, but must at a minimum include transit fare collection, parking payment and electronic toll collection."

The RFP also informed proposers that a separately funded evaluation of the project would be undertaken by a third party contractor, and that the participating agencies would be required to participate in and support the evaluation effort.

2.1 Participants and Management Structure

The ORANGES partnership involved both public and private sector participants:

- **Public Sector Partners:** The Central Florida Regional Transportation Authority (doing business as LYNX), the Orlando-Orange County Expressway Authority (OOCEA) and the City of Orlando were the Public Agency Partners, with LYNX also serving as the Federal grantee and manager of the FOT. The following individuals were the primary representatives for the Public Sector Partners on the evaluation team:

  - Doug Jamison, LYNX

  - David Wynne, OOCEA

  - Pamela Corbin, City of Orlando Parking Bureau

- **Private Sector Partners:** Private sector firms implemented the FOT system under contract, on behalf of the Public Partners. Post Buckley Schuh & Jernigan (PBS&J) was

---

[5] This was originally released in 1999 as the "Request for Proposals for an Operational Test of an Electronic Payment System for Transportation and Other Applications", building on an earlier "Request for Letters of Interest to Participate in an Operational Test of an Electronic Payment System for Transit Fare Collection and Other Applications" released in 1998.

contracted to LYNX as its General ITS & APTS Consultant, with FOT responsibilities including program management, oversight and implementation support. TranSend[6] was the Lead Technical Partner responsible for system development and integration, implementing and operating the clearinghouse – also contracted to LYNX. Other Technical Partners joining the implementation team later were AnswerSearch (cardholder recruitment), Alliance Data Systems (merchant acquiring services for credit card transaction processing) and E-Squared Engineering (customer service strategy and brochures). Additional services and equipment suppliers included Suntrust Bank (Automated Clearing House, or ACH, transfers of settlement funds), Ascom Transport Systems (transit smart card validators), EFKON (toll plaza readers and smart card accepting transponder equipment), Gemplus (dual interface smart cards) and McGann Parking Systems (parking garage readers). Ascom, EFKON and McGann provided equipment as well as some installation, configuration and integration effort for free or at reduced cost to assist the goals of the FOT.

2.2 FOT Overview

The FOT implemented a central payment and clearinghouse system using core technology from TranSend. Payment transactions completed at smart card readers operated by individual agencies were transmitted to the ORANGES clearinghouse for settlement to agency-owned revenue accounts.

The scope of the FOT involved a limited scale test demonstration under revenue service conditions:

- **Card base:** A single card could be loaded with multiple payment applications, thus allowing the card to be accepted for payment across all agencies. The agencies intended to maintain 800-1200 smart cards in active use at all times during the test. However, during the demonstration, the active card base[7] remained below 160.

- **Transit component:** LYNX equipped two (2) routes; Links 13 and 15. Each of these routes connected post-secondary educational institutions with the downtown area.

- **Toll component:** The Orlando-Orange County Expressway Authority (OOCEA) equipped selected lanes of the Holland East toll plaza on State Route 408 to accept the EFKON transponder with a smart card, as well as installed "Touch and Go" smart card accepting validators, in selected manual lanes for each direction. Smart card acceptance through transponders in five lanes (two in each direction plus one reversible lane) was

---

[6] During the demonstration, Touch Technology International was reorganized, and the part of the original organization responsible for supporting the demonstration became known as TranSend.

[7] A card became classified as active once first used, but subsequently classified as inactive if not used for three consecutive weeks.

deferred one or two months from the FOT launch. The Holland East plaza is a 14-lane facility. Lanes 1-7 operate westbound, lanes 9-14 operate eastbound, and lane 8 is reversible. This plaza accounts for approximately 20% of the revenue and transactions annually for OOCEA.

- **Parking component:** The City of Orlando Parking Bureau equipped cashier booths in the Central Boulevard, Library and Market Street garages.

- **Revaluing facilities:** Each agency offered facilities for smart card issuance and revaluing. This included points of sale at agency-operated customer service facilities, selected attended toll lanes and parking garage exits, and some locations operated by third parties (additional details on revaluing locations and payment methods accepted are provided below). Transit passes continued to be sold only through LYNX facilities, and transponders continued to be available only through OOCEA facilities.

The system test configuration strategy was specifically designed to isolate the smart card payment system from the existing legacy systems where necessary in the operation at each agency. This strategy provided the least risk to existing operations and revenue management.

Card-based stored value, or electronic cash, was stored in a "purse" application on the card and accepted as a form of payment across all agencies (equipped LYNX buses, City parking garages and OOCEA "Touch and Go" toll lanes), with the payment value deducted from the card-based stored value balance at the point of purchase. The expiration date of a monthly LYNX pass could also be stored on the card. The OOCEA account-based stored value balance was stored at the clearinghouse. The plaza lane equipment communicated with the smart card (via the transponder) to identify the account as it passed through. The toll payment was then deducted from the account. If a LYNX pass expired or a toll account developed insufficient value, the card/account in question was included on an updated "hotlist" that was sent to the card reading equipment prohibiting use of the pass or account until properly revalued.

2.3 OOCEA

Rather than integrate the existing E-PASS Electronic Toll Collection (ETC) system with the smart card clearinghouse, OOCEA opted to create a parallel ETC system in equipped lanes, using EFKON smart card accepting transponders and smart card readers.

Figure 1: Transponder that Accepts Smart Cards

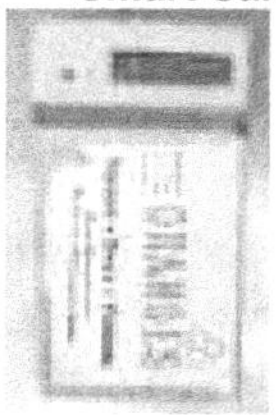

Source: ORANGES Consortium

Smart Card Accepting Transponders

The OOCEA customer service center distributed the EFKON smart card accepting transponders in addition to conventional transponders (see Figure 1). Customers inserted the smart card into the EFKON transponder to have their toll fees deducted from their ORANGES toll account held at the central clearinghouse. The toll account operation was similar to the EPASS account already offered by the OOCEA to its customers.

EFKON transponders used infrared communications with the laneside readers and communicated with EFKON controllers in the toll plaza. The EFKON system was integrated with the clearinghouse, bypassing the existing ETC system. OOCEA customers that received EFKON transponders continued to use their conventional transponder for non-equipped toll lanes. The conventional transponder was also read by the Holland East plaza equipment, which activated the "paid" laneside signal (the OOCEA account was also charged in the process, but this was reversed out when there was a corresponding payment from the ORANGES account).

Smart Card Validators

Selected manual lanes were also equipped with EFKON validators (see Figure 2), similar to those used for payments on the LYNX buses. The validators allowed customers to pay tolls using electronic cash stored on the smart card by stopping and placing the smart card in proximity to the validator mounted in the lane. The smart card was thus an alternative to tossing coins into the automated coin machines in the unattended cash lanes. The EFKON lane controller was integrated with the existing lane violation system. Therefore, after the card was presented for payment, the completed payment triggered a green light signaling the driver to proceed.

Figure 2: Toll Lane Smart Card Validator

Source: ORANGES Consortium

2.4 LYNX

All LYNX buses have registering fareboxes, which the agency had recently replaced with a new model. Integration of smart card readers into this new farebox was impractical from both a schedule and budget standpoint for the FOT. The ORANGES partners therefore opted for stand-alone validators from Ascom Transport Systems (see Figure 3) to stay within budget and schedule constraints. These units were mounted beside the fareboxes but not integrated with them. The ORANGES card could be used as an alternative to either cash fare payment or the LYNX paper monthly pass.

Figure 3: Stand-Alone Transit Smart Card Validator

Source: ORANGES Consortium

2.5 City of Orlando Parking Bureau

Selected garages accepted the ORANGES card using a smart card reader that had been integrated into a free-standing housing by McGann Software Systems; this reader supported both proximity and swipe card technology (see Figure 4). The ORANGES card provided an alternative to the need for the hourly parker to pick up an entry ticket to mark the duration of time in the garage to determine the payment amount upon exit.

Figure 4: Parking Garage Validator

Source: ORANGES Consortium

Instead, the smart card was presented to the McGann reader upon garage entry and exit for fee calculation. The cash value stored on the card was debited for payment upon calculation of the parking fee. The transaction data was transferred to the ORANGES clearinghouse after being consolidated by the Parking revenue management system. At the request of the Parking Bureau, participation in the FOT was restricted to hourly/daily customers and did not include monthly parking patrons, who use an existing parking proximity card.

2.6 Smart Card Issuance and Revaluing

Issuance, Distribution and Revaluing

Cards were initialized centrally, and distributed to cardholders by mail. A cardholder then used one of the revaluing points to add value to the electronic purse or to purchase a LYNX transit pass and load it onto the card. Replacement cards were still initialized centrally, and then distributed either by mail or through one of the revaluing locations. Table 1 summarizes the revaluing locations that were available and the payment methods accepted at each. Some automatic revaluing arrangements were also available:

- LYNX offered an automatic pass renewal service. Customers registered by providing a credit card number, which was used to automatically renew a pass five days prior to its scheduled expiration. The clearinghouse automatically requested a credit authorization on the registered account for the amount of the new transit pass. This pass renewal was then updated on the card when used at a LYNX validator as long as a positive authorization had been received on the purchase request. The original pass on the card continued to be used up until its expiration date before the next purchased pass was used for fare payment. If a successful authorization could not be obtained, the existing pass on the card continued in use until it expired.

- OOCEA offered automatic toll account replenishment of funds via a registered credit card. As tolls were paid, funds were moved from the customer toll account to agency revenue. The clearinghouse automatically generated a credit card purchase request for $20 to replenish the account whenever the balance dropped to $5 or less. If a successful credit card authorization could not be obtained, the transponder that had been issued was hot-listed once existing funds were depleted, to prevent further use until funds could be replenished.

Table 1. Revaluing Locations and Payment Methods Accepted

Agency	Revaluing Location	Payment Methods Accepted		
		Cash	Check	Credit Card
Parking Bureau	Central Boulevard Garage – Cashier Booth	✔	✔	✔
	Central Boulevard Garage – Payment Office	✔	✔	✔
	Market Garage – Cashier Booth	✔	✔	✔
	Library Garage – Cashier Booth	✔	✔	✔
LYNX	Downtown Bus Terminal – Sales Window	✔	✔	✔
	Valencia Community College East – Book Store	✔	✔	✔
	University of Central Florida – Student Union Ticket Office	✔		
OOCEA	Holland East Toll Plaza – Designated Staffed Lanes	✔		
	East Side Service Center	✔	✔	✔

Cardholder Participation Incentives

The agencies offered several cardholder participation incentives:

- LYNX cardholders received a 15% discount on single ride, weekly and monthly fares (e.g., $1.06 instead of $1.25 for a single ride);

- Parking customers received 50% off hourly and daily parking fees; and

- Initial OOCEA customers received a smart card with $5 preloaded, and a $20 check at the end of the 12-month trial if they remained an active user throughout the FOT period. This incentive was discontinued after issuance of the initial 300 cards by OOCEA, as it was determined that many customers discontinued use of the smart card once the initial five dollars was used.

2.7 Clearinghouse

The primary role of a clearinghouse is to process all of the transactions in the payment system according to business rules established by the members and to settle funds among the participating agencies. Settlement is the creation of the accounting entries, and this action was done daily by the ORANGES system. Funds movement, however, was a separate action that occurred bi-monthly in the ORANGES project. This decision was made by the partners to reduce the cost of bank fees for ACH due to the limited scale of the FOT. In the ORANGES project, the clearinghouse also performed two important additional functions. It facilitated (1) all transit pass purchases by credit card and (2) all load processing to electronic cash stored on the card or to toll accounts.

The ORANGES clearinghouse also played a unique role for LYNX in this implementation by providing all software and revenue management processing of the smart card transactions performed for transit. This "front-end" role is not generally handled by a clearinghouse, but is instead typically done by the transit agency itself using software provided by the fare system hardware vendor. In ORANGES, though, Ascom Transport Services provided only the bus validator and collector hardware devices, but no operating software. Therefore, the clearinghouse system performed both front-end and back-end processing for LYNX during this FOT.

In ORANGES, settlement processing was based upon the type of payment application, the owner of the application (including considering whether the application was shared among participants) and the issuer of the card. Settlement of payment applications can be very straightforward or quite complex, depending on the nature of the business rules. In the ORANGES project, LYNX was the only transit agency. Therefore, all transit pass sales were handled by LYNX or its contracted agents, and all of the funds generated from transit pass sales were simply deposited by the clearinghouse into the LYNX revenue account.

On the other hand, the settlement of payments made with electronic cash required the clearinghouse to know the issuer of the card and the owner of the reader where the payment was made. If, for example, a cardholder was issued a card from LYNX and loaded $30 into the electronic purse on the card, these funds were held by LYNX in an account called a funds pool until the electronic cash was used for payment. If during a certain settlement period, the LYNX card was used to make $3 in toll payments at OOCEA and $1 in payments at parking garages, the clearinghouse would execute the settlement by transferring these amounts from the LYNX account to the bank (revenue) accounts of the other agencies. If the card was used to pay, say, $1.06 for a bus ride, the clearinghouse would transfer funds from the LYNX funds pool to the LYNX revenue account. Alternatively, if the LYNX cardholder made his/her initial load or revaluing payment at a revaluing device operated by another agency, the funds were initially placed in the account of the agency that received the load/revaluing payment from the cardholder. The settlement process was then used to transfer the funds to LYNX (i.e., after the cardholder used the card to ride LYNX).

In the ORANGES project, the agencies were free to establish the accounting instructions that the clearinghouse should use in the settlement process. Both the OOCEA and the City of Orlando chose to use a single bank account for settlement, but to utilize reporting from the clearinghouse to make the appropriate internal account entries for revenue and for value held in the funds pool. LYNX opted to maintain two separate bank accounts during this project, one for holding the funds pool that had not yet been used by the cardholders for purchases, the other for holding funds received for pass purchases and collected transit fares.

The various funds movements in and out of each agency account with daily settlement were consolidated into net transfers through the use of a clearing account. Funds movement occurred every two weeks. Table 2 provides sample reconciliation information that summarizes the derivation of the net settlement payments.

2.8 Implementation Schedule

The FOT system design and development used the following approach (Figure 5 illustrates the planned and actual implementation schedules):

- *Planned Pilot Development:* The pilot version of the system, demonstrating the integration of all equipment and subsystems in a laboratory-testing environment, was to have been developed during the initial 11 months (i.e., April 2001 through February 2002).

- *Actual Pilot Development:* This stage of development actually took place over the 26 months between April 2001 and May 2003. This pilot system created a prototype of the revenue service system in a laboratory-testing environment. Much more time than anticipated was spent on addressing various design and resource availability issues.

- *Planned FOT Development:* A partial FOT test configuration was scheduled to have been completed, fully tested and brought into revenue service between March 2002 and September 2002, and the full FOT test configuration completed by February 2003. Hence, the FOT development, from completing the initial pilot through completing FOT test configuration , was to have spanned a 12-month period from March 2002 through February 2003.

- *Actual FOT Development:* The full FOT test configuration was initiated prior to the completion of the pilot, in May 2003, and brought into revenue service only 2 months later, at the beginning of August 2003. At that time, some functionality was not initially in place – in particular the toll accounts processing needed to support the smart card accepting transponders. The full functionality of the system was deemed operational by the agencies as of January 2004, and was operational through the end of July 2004.

Table 2. Sample Clearinghouse Settlement Activity

E-CASH ACTIVITY AND SOURCE

	LYNX		OOCEA		City Parking		Net To/From Funds Pool
LYNX	$ (1.00)	$ 36.50	$ (0.75)	$ -	$ -	$ -	$ 34.75
OOCEA	$ (0.75)	$ -	$ (341.79)	$ 780.05	$ (2.50)	$ -	$ 435.01
City	$ (3.00)	$ -	$ (26.25)	$ 50.00	$ (114.50)	$ 424.19	$ 330.44
	$ (4.75)	$ 36.50	$ (368.79)	$ 830.05	$ (117.00)	$ 424.19	$ 800.20

Accounts

LYNX Funds Pool

$ (1.00)	To LYNX Revenue for e-cash purchases
$ (277.10)	To LYNX Revenue for pass purchases
$ (0.75)	To OOCEA for purchases
$ (278.85)	**Net to Clearing Account**

LYNX Revenue

$ 1.00	From LYNX FP for e-cash purchases
$ 277.10	From LYNX FP for pass purchases
$ 0.75	From OOCEA for purchases
$ 3.00	From City for purchases
$ 281.85	**Net from Clearing Account**

OOCEA

$ 0.75	From LYNX FP for purchases
$ 26.25	From City for purchases
$ (0.75)	To LYNX Revenue for purchases
$ (2.50)	To City for purchases
$ (50.00)	To City for loads
$ (26.25)	**Net to Clearing Account**

City Parking

$ 2.50	From OOCEA for purchases
$ 50.00	From OOCEA for Loads
$ (3.00)	To LYNX Revenue for purchases
$ (26.25)	To OOCEA for purchases
$ 23.25	**Net from Clearing Account**

$ (305.10)	**Total credits to Clearing Account**
$ 305.10	**Total debits to Clearing Account**

Overall, development of the full test configuration was to have been completed over the 23 months between April 2001 and February 2003. This effort was actually completed (with the exception of functionality deferred until January 2004, such as the toll accounts processing for smart card accepting transponders) over a 28 month period between April 2001 and the beginning of August 2003.

Figure 5. Planned and Actual Test Configuration Development Timelines

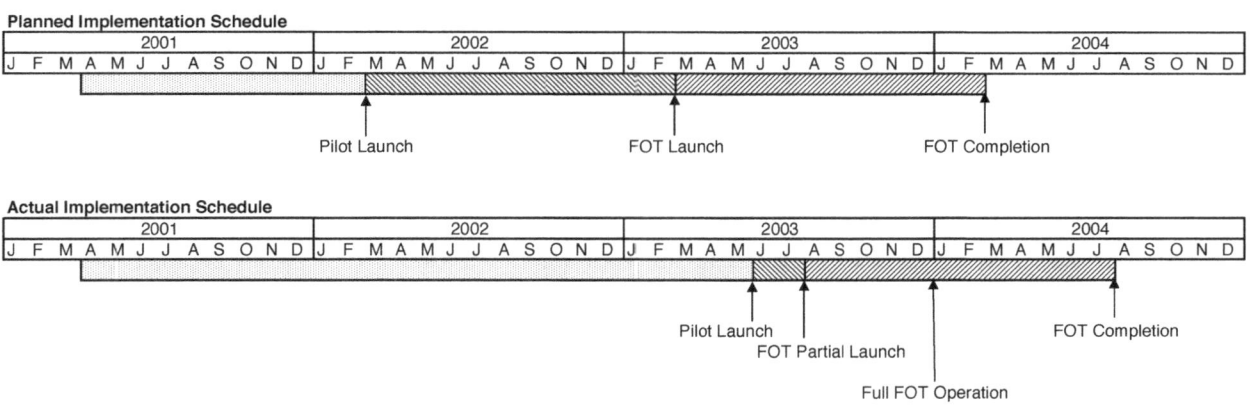

3 Evaluation Strategy and Plan

3.1 US DOT Evaluation Process

As part of the ITS program, US DOT requires that each FOT have an independent evaluator. This national evaluation is a supplementary effort to the locally funded and managed FOT self-evaluation. The national evaluation is separately funded and has independent goals, objectives, schedule and deliverables. The US DOT evaluations also provide useful feedback to the local FOT participants, as well as other interested transportation stakeholders.

For further details, please refer to the TEA-21 Evaluation Guidelines, www.its.dot.gov/eval/ResourceGuide (originally published in the Federal Register). A brief overview of some key material from the Guidelines is provided below for ready reference – together with the approach used in the ORANGES evaluation:

- US DOT program assessment has a dual focus:

  - **Outputs:** The evaluation documents *what was done* in the FOT (e.g., systems built, the capabilities provided, institutional arrangements). The background description of the ORANGES system provided in Section 1 of this report provides this documentation.

  - **Outcomes:** The evaluation documents *what was achieved* through the FOT, relative to a set of goals and measures established in collaboration with the local participants early in the effort. Goals and measures have been developed by consensus for the ORANGES evaluation – as discussed in Section 3.3 of this report.

- The federal Evaluation Guidelines define a common process for both the US DOT and local evaluations, and this process was followed for this evaluation:

  - **Establish the Evaluation Team:** Evaluation team members included participants from all local FOT participants (public and private sector partners) as well as representatives from the US DOT evaluation team[8]. The ORANGES evaluation team included the core public agency partners as well as the lead private sector partners.

  - **Develop the Evaluation Strategy and Plan:** The evaluation team established the goals and measures that were the focus of the evaluation. Each goal with a quantifiable measure was framed as a testable hypothesis – involving a statement

---

[8] The US DOT Evaluation Team for the ORANGES Evaluation was led by the Federal Transit Administration and the Volpe National Transportation Systems Center, with technical support from TranSystems Corp.

about a potential benefit the FOT was expected to provide. The need to support the evaluation of certain goals with a qualitative assessment was also considered. In these cases, measurement involved monitoring the evolution of opinion for various groups of FOT participants (e.g., customers and/or employees) through discussion groups -- without any particular hypothesis.

- **Develop Test Plans:** For each testable hypothesis and qualitative assessment, a plan was defined for gathering data on the associated measure. This included defining desired opportunities to gather data for the before vs. after – and/or test vs. control – dimensions.

- **Data Collection and Analysis:** The quantitative and qualitative data required by the test plans was collected – and used for qualitative assessments and comparison with the testable hypotheses. The role of the initial data collection was to gather "baseline" data about initial conditions before the FOT system was in place. The remainder of the data collection occurred after the FOT system had been implemented.

- **Document the Evaluation:** The strategy, plans, results, conclusions and recommendations were ultimately combined into an **Evaluation Final Report** (this document).

3.2 Developing Consensus on the Evaluation Goals and Measures

The process for developing consensus on an initial set of evaluation goals and measures was completed in collaboration with the ORANGES partners – and included the following steps:

- Generating a list of potential goals and measures based on input from the partners. These were discussed with the partners, including how data could be collected.

- Soliciting input from each partner independently on relative priorities for the goals.

- Developing consensus with the partners on the initial set of evaluation goals and measures.

The starting point for this consensus building effort was a set of goals and measures proposed by the USDOT evaluation team. These were developed based on the priority input received from the partners as well as the following additional considerations:

- Consistency with goals of the federal ITS program.[9]

- A <u>clearly</u> associated benefit and measure.

- A *feasible and reasonable data collection* method for the measure, consistent with the scale and duration of the FOT.

Feasible and reasonable data collection generally corresponds to measures for which either:

- Quantitative data can be provided by the operating agencies (or derived from data that can be provided).

- Qualitative input can be gathered from discussion groups whose participation can be arranged by the operating agencies.

3.3 Evaluation Goals, Measures and Test Hypotheses

Tables 3 and 4 identify the set of quantitative and qualitative goals and measures initially established for the evaluation, as developed through the consensus-building process. The tables also list the fundamental test hypothesis for each quantitative goal and measure. This initial consensus created the basis to develop test plans and investigate sources for the baseline data collection effort.

3.4 Test Plans

The test plans were developed to address the data collection and analysis methods to support the evaluation of the goals, measures and test hypotheses are presented in Appendix A.

---

[9] The following National ITS goals are cited in the Guidelines: (1) traveler safety; (2) traveler mobility; (3) transportation system efficiency; (4) productivity of transportation providers; (5) conservation of energy and protection of the environment; and (6) others as may be appropriate to unique features of the project.

Table 3: Quantitative Evaluation Goals/Measures and Test Hypotheses

FOT Evaluation Goal	Measure	Test Hypothesis
1. Increase parking revenue	• Revenue received	• Revenue will increase from parking payment equipment that accepts smart cards, due to increased equipment availability and improved customer convenience. The degree of revenue increase will vary for different types of parking equipment.
2. Increase transponder market penetration	• Number of smart card users that newly acquire a transponder	• Of the smart card users, some will choose to newly acquire a transponder
3. Reduce transaction times	• Average transaction times	• Smart card transactions will be quicker than cash payment, so average time will reduce if there is a shift from cash to smart card.
4. Increase prepaid revenue share	• % revenue prepaid	• The % of revenue that is prepaid will increase for equipment that accepts smart cards
5. Reduce monthly pass distribution costs	• Procurement, inventory, delivery, commissions for any conventional passes made available on smart cards	• The number of conventional passes being distributed will decrease, thus reducing distribution costs
6. Increase automated payment equipment uptime	• % equipment availability	• The decreased use of cash will improve equipment reliability
7. Cardholders use the joint account[10]	• Card use profiles • Average prepaid balance • Modal use profile	• Customers that activate joint transportation accounts will maintain a prepaid balance and use the card frequently. Multimodal use by individual cardholders will most often involve tolls and parking.

[10] The joint account involved the ability to use one or more different types of smart card with smart card readers installed at transit, parking and toll facilities. The joint account did not involve use of the same account for both smart cards and toll transponders.

Table 4: Qualitative Goals/Measures and Test Hypotheses

FOT Evaluation Goal	Measure
8. Understand customer perceptions • **General benefits** • **Ease of use** • **Convenience of revaluing**	• Customer feedback
9. Understand operations/maintenance staff perceptions, including: • **General benefits** • **Reduced payment disputes** • **Reduced transfer abuse** • **Ease of customer use** • **Maintenance**	• Operations/maintenance staff feedback
10. Understand planning/management staff perceptions, including: • **General benefits** • **More comprehensive data collection**	• Planning/management staff feedback
11. Understand interagency perceptions, including: • **General institutional issues** • **Interagency collaboration**	• Partnership feedback

4 Before Data Analysis for Quantitative Goals

4.1 Quantitative Goal 4 – Reduce Transaction Times

Reducing average transaction times is important for all three modes and can translate directly into reduced queuing and bus dwell times. This quantitative goal was not applied to tolls for the evaluation, since the percentage paying by transponder or smart card would not noticeably increase within the high volume of daily plaza transactions.

Measure

- Average payment transaction duration, for each mode and type of equipment.

Test Hypothesis

- Since prepaid payment transactions will be quicker than cash payment, the average duration will decrease if the % prepaid increases.

Data Collection and Analysis

Parking

At each of the three equipped parking garages (Central Boulevard, Library and Market), a Parking Bureau observer recorded the duration for a sample of payment transactions at the cashier booth. The transaction time was the length of time the vehicle was stopped at the booth.

Table 5 summarizes the sample size, average, standard deviation, and precision percentage for each of these samples. The confidence intervals on the average for each garage were similar enough that it seemed reasonable to combine the garages together into a single large sample. For all garages together, we make the following statistical statement:

- Three garages combined: At the 95% confidence level, the average transaction time was expected to be 23.3 s +/- 5% (i.e., between 22.1 and 24.5 seconds, 95% of the time).

Transit

On buses for each of the two equipped LYNX bus routes (Links 13 and 15), the Automatic Passenger Counting (APC) equipment was used to gather data during selected weeks when these buses were in use on these routes (only a subset of the LYNX bus fleet is APC-equipped). The APC equipment recorded at each stop the number of passengers that boarded and alighted as well as the duration the doors were open.

Several data filtering steps were taken to help construct samples where the duration the doors were open could be divided by the number of boarding passengers at that stop to best represent the average transaction time per boarding passenger at that stop:

- LYNX filtered out stops entries that were time points/layovers (either due to it being a known characteristic of the stop, excessive dwell time or having no passenger activity), or for some other reason might have involved the doors being open longer than needed for passenger movement alone.

Table 5. Statistical Analysis of Parking Transaction Times Data

Garage	Sample Date	Sample Size	Average (s)	Standard Deviation (s)	Precision
Central Boulevard Garage	1/15	60	23.4	20.4	22%
	2/20	60	23.9	13.4	14%
	3/17	60	22.7	15.2	17%
	4/14	60	23.3	22.1	24%
	5/16	60	18.8	7.5	10%
	Combined	300	22.4	16.5	8%
Library Garage	1/16	60	22.1	8.6	10%
	2/18	60	25.6	10.1	10%
	3/20	60	19.8	18.2	23%
	4/25	60	25.9	17.0	17%
	5/28	62	25.4	12.8	13%
	Combined	302	23.8	14.0	7%
Market Garage	1/16	60	24.2	12.5	13%
	2/20	60	25.6	44.9	44%
	3/18	60	23.4	10.1	11%
	4/24	60	24.9	17.6	18%
	5/14	62	20.2	17.2	21%
	Combined	302	23.6	23.9	11%
All Garages Combined		904	23.3	18.6	5%

- An additional filtering step by the evaluation team removed any remaining stop entries that involved at least 120 seconds per boarding passenger. It was assumed that these represented unrecognized delays beyond what was needed to board passengers (e.g., timepoints/layovers). This was a judgment in the sense that all longer durations per passenger (e.g., greater than about 30 seconds per passenger) might be of this type. On the other hand, some of these longer durations could be legitimately associated with a boarding passenger (e.g., trouble finding change or a fare dispute). Implicit in the test hypothesis is the expectation that the smart card would tend to reduce the incidence of longer fare payment events. So, retaining the somewhat longer duration stop entries in the samples (i.e., the longer ones that are less than 120 seconds) is intended to capture situations that may be mitigated by the smart card.

- The evaluation team noted that some stop entries seemed infeasible (e.g., several people boarding within 1-2 seconds). This could indicate variations in the behavior of the APC equipment (e.g., over counting boardings, undercounting the duration of the door opening). Since there is no reason to believe that the underlying cause of these is limited only to these stop entries, these have not been eliminated from the sample so as to avoid introducing a bias against short duration stop entries. It was assumed that these effects were prevalent to a similar degree in the before and after testing (i.e., so that they balance out in the before vs. after comparison).

- Passengers simultaneously board (through the front door) and alight (through the rear door). LYNX filtered out stop entries where the number of alighting passengers exceeded the number boarding, in which case the duration of the doors being open would not have been governed by the number of boarding passengers.

- An additional filtering step undertaken by the evaluation team was to remove stop entries listing a dwell time of zero, since these entries apparently represent faulty data.

Table 6 summarizes the sample size, average, standard deviation, and precision percentage for each of these samples. Sample sizes provided by LYNX differed considerably relative to the time periods covered. On some dates some APC data was missing, which accounts for these differences – although these occurrences were random and each sample should still remain representative (i.e., similar averages in the various samples). The confidence intervals on the average for each route were distinct enough that it seemed reasonable to not combine the routes together into a single large sample. For these routes, we were able to make the following statistical statements:

- Link 13: At the 95% confidence level, the average transaction time was expected to be 13.0 s +/- 4% (i.e., between 12.5 and 13.5 seconds, 95% of the time).

- Link 15: At the 95% confidence level, the average transaction time was expected to be 10.6 s +/- 3% (i.e., between 10.3 and 10.9 seconds, 95% of the time).

4.2 Quantitative Goal 5 – Increase Prepaid Revenue Share

In general, operating agencies wish to (1) reduce cash handling costs and (2) increase the "float" investment revenue earned from holding prepaid revenue. However, changes in cash handling costs and float revenue were not expected here due to the limited scale of the FOT test configuration. Prepaid revenue share was selected as a measurable surrogate quantitative goal for equipped facilities. It was therefore necessary to determine whether some of the ORANGES card usage was displaced from other prepaid payment methods rather than from cash. For this reason, we looked at the overall percentage using any prepaid method, rather than only the percentage using the ORANGES card. This goal was not applied to tolls for the evaluation, since the percentage paying by transponder would not noticeably increase within the high volume of daily plaza transactions.

Table 6. Statistical Analysis of Transit Transaction Times Data

Bus Route	Sample Date	Sample Size	Average (s)	Standard Deviation (s)	Precision
Link 13	12/2-12/6	79	9.7	10.4	23%
	12/9-12/13	303	13.0	11.2	10%
	1/26-2/1	686	12.8	13.7	8%
	4/1-4/14	275	14.6	19.1	15%
	6/25-6/30	920	12.9	13.3	7%
	Combined	2263	13.0	13.9	4%
Link 15	12/2-12/6	490	10.3	7.4	6%
	12/9-12/13	442	10.5	7.6	7%
	1/26-2/1	569	10.8	11.6	9%
	4/1-4/14	275	11.6	11.2	11%
	6/11-6/17	119	11.8	9.2	14%
	6/20-6/30	933	10.2	7.5	5%
	Combined	2828	10.6	9.0	3%

Measure

- % of transactions that use a prepaid revenue payment method

Test Hypothesis

- % prepaid transactions will increase for equipment accepting the ORANGES card

Data Collection and Analysis

Parking

The Parking Bureau was able to provide monthly summaries for each parking garage over the period from October 2002 through March 2003, indicating the amounts received for the following types of parking payment methods:

- Monthly parking permits – a prepaid method;

- Transient parking – cash payment at the exit cashier booth;

- Evening parking – cash payment on entry during the evening hours, so that the exit cashier booth can be unattended.

Table 7 presents this data (rounded to the nearest dollar). For each garage, the percent prepaid varied from month to month, so an overall percentage was not calculated for each garage. Instead, a statistical analysis was performed:

- Central Boulevard Garage: At the 95% confidence level, the average prepaid revenue share was expected to be 52% +/- 12% (i.e., between 45% and 58%, 95% of the time).

- Library Garage: At the 95% confidence level, the average prepaid revenue share was expected to be 46% +/- 16% (i.e., between 39% and 53%, 95% of the time).

- Market Garage: At the 95% confidence level, the average prepaid revenue share was expected to be 47% +/- 14% (i.e., between 40% and 54%, 95% of the time).

Table 7. Parking Prepaid Revenue Share Data

Garage	Month	Prepaid	Cash	Total	Prepaid Revenue Share
Central Boulevard	October	$84,863	$51,390	$136,253	62%
	November	$69,492	$45,561	$115,053	60%
	December	$56,709	$69,174	$125,883	45%
	January	$63,953	$59,772	$123,726	52%
	February	$57,552	$61,458	$119,010	48%
	March	$58,530	$77,712	$136,241	43%
Library	October	$43,739	$36,146	$79,885	55%
	November	$27,363	$33,567	$60,930	45%
	December	$44,029	$40,579	$84,608	52%
	January	$42,292	$37,073	$79,364	53%
	February	$26,764	$52,989	$79,753	34%
	March	$32,961	$58,696	$91,657	36%
Market	October	$15,228	$24,827	$40,055	38%
	November	$19,446	$25,726	$45,172	43%
	December	$22,040	$28,643	$50,682	43%
	January	$20,776	$26,132	$46,909	44%
	February	$6,606	$5,348	$11,953	55%
	March	$15,632	$11,075	$26,708	59%

Transit

LYNX was able to provide monthly summaries for the fareboxes on each route for the period from November 2002 through March 2003, indicating the percent of the ridership using the following categories of transit payment methods:

- Prepaid – passes, tickets and transfers – and free rides;

- Cash

Table 8 presents this data. The data represents the prepaid share of the ridership, rather than the prepaid share of the revenue (i.e., the prepaid revenue share would be somewhat lower, given the lower average fare for prepaid riders). On December 28, 2002, LYNX introduced a new fare structure that replaced calendar weekly period passes with activate-on-first-use 7 day period passes, and added a day pass. As one would expect, these new fare options have shown a tendency to increase the prepaid ridership share. Since this share was in transition during the before data collection period, an overall percentage was not calculated for each route. Instead, a statistical analysis was performed for the data beginning in January 2003:

- Link 13: At the 95% confidence level, the average prepaid ridership share was expected to be 58% +/- 3% (i.e., between 57% and 60%, 95% of the time).

- Link 15: At the 95% confidence level, the average prepaid ridership share was expected to be 57% +/- 2% (i.e., between 56% and 58%, 95% of the time).

Table 8. Transit Prepaid Ridership Share Data

Route	Month	Prepaid	Cash	Total	Prepaid Ridership Share
Link 13	November	18,104	18,951	37,055	49%
	December	15,680	16,306	31,986	49%
	January	20,942	16,020	36,962	57%
	February	21,332	15,449	36,781	58%
	March	22,222	14,864	37,086	60%
Link 15	November	21,515	23,471	44,986	48%
	December	19,853	22,929	42,782	46%
	January	26,604	20,321	46,925	57%
	February	25,537	19,966	45,503	56%
	March	26,433	18,950	45,383	58%

4.3 Quantitative Goal 6 – Increase Automated Payment Equipment Uptime

Typically, cash accepting equipment suffers more downtime as the cash volume increases. This applies more to unattended automated devices than to attended locations, since these devices use mechanical methods to automate cash acceptance. By displacing cash use, the ORANGES card should reduce downtime. This would reduce maintenance costs and revenue loss (i.e., at unattended devices where revenue cannot be collected while the device is down).

Measure

- % of operating hours with cash processing available (i.e., coins for toll Automatic Coin Machines, or ACMs, and coins and bills for fareboxes)

Test Hypothesis

- The frequency and severity of planned and unplanned maintenance for unattended devices relates to the amount of cash processed. Cash processing availability should increase as % prepaid increases.

Data Collection and Analysis

Tolls

OOCEA was able to provide data on the times when the various lanes at the Holland East toll plaza were down due to a failure attributed to "ACM and tunnel vault" (see Table 9). ACM failures were expected to be a frequent occurrence in this category. This data was provided for the entire months from November 2002 through March 2003.

Table 9. Toll Lanes Automated Coin Machine Uptime Data

Month	Downtime (DD:HH:MM)	Availability
November	00:18:09	99.4%
December	00:19:14	99.4%
January	00:12:35	99.6%
February	01:11:16	98.7%
March	00:07:30	99.8%
Combined	03:20:44	99.4%

Only lanes 4 and 5 (westbound) and lanes 10 and 11 (eastbound) were equipped with ACMs. The percentage availability calculation was based on the fact that these four lanes operate continuously. For the purposes of the evaluation, combining the data for the 5-month period enhances the overall value of the percentage availability. The statistical assessment for this 5-month sample indicates:

- At the 95% confidence level, the average ACM % availability was expected to be 99.38% +/- 0.37% (i.e., between 99.02% and 99.74%, 95% of the time).

Transit

LYNX was able to provide data on the durations for which the farebox was not in service each day, for the ten fareboxes that were equipped for ORANGES acceptance, for the period November 2002 through March 2003 (see Table 10). Combining this with the duration of service each day for the equipped vehicles allows the farebox % availability to be calculated for each month. The specific cause of the various farebox downtime incidents was not available from this data, although it is generally known that problems with the cash accepting components and power supply were common causes of farebox incidents.

In this case, combining the data for the 5 months enhances the overall value of the percentage availability. These durations have been combined for the ten fareboxes. The statistical assessment for this 5-month sample indicates:

- At the 95% confidence level, the average farebox % availability was expected to be 99.12% +/- 0.19% (i.e., between 98.93% and 99.31%, 95% of the time).

Table 10. Transit Farebox Uptime Data

Month	Scheduled for Operation (DD:HH:MM)	Operational (DD:HH:MM)	Availability
November	180:10:45	179:7:51	99.4%
December	186:21:52	185:14:47	99.3%
January	185:21:13	183:23:02	99.0%
February	168:00:32	166:07:59	99.0%
March	186:21:43	184:19:48	98.9%
Combined	913:04:05	905:01:27	99.1%

4.4 Quantitative Goal 8 – Characterize Current Pass Distribution and Permit Billing Costs

LYNX uses prepaid fares extensively, issuing paper and magnetic stripe passes that are distributed through 81 sales outlets and by mail order. For the FOT, LYNX passes were renewed directly on the smart card using revaluing locations at three of the existing sales outlets. Sales locations should therefore have needed fewer paper passes, which should have provided some savings. The ORANGES card may also eventually replace the monthly "proximity" permit for garage parking. Currently, permit holders are billed monthly. Although this capability was not included in the FOT test configuration, a permit could be automatically renewed and the cost billed to a pre-registered credit card.

However, any reduction in the number of passes distributed was limited during the test (and permits continued to be billed using conventional methods). Characterizing the current costs for pass distribution and permit billing, though, should indicate the magnitude of the potential cost savings if bigger reductions were achieved through future full-scale deployment. The specific cost categories and assumptions included have been documented for use in any such future consideration of this data. (This goal was not applied to tolls, which already use a transponder and autoload.)

Measure

- Costs for monthly billing of garage permits.

- Costs for distributing conventional weekly and monthly passes.

Data Collection and Analysis

Parking

The Parking Bureau assembled average monthly costs for processing monthly permit invoices. The Parking Bureau included in the cost:

- Salary/benefits cost for the accounting clerk performing this function;

- Postage costs for mailing the invoices.

Table 11 summarizes this data.

Table 11. Parking Permit Invoice Processing Costs

Accounting Clerk Salary/Benefits ($/hour)	$20.19
Average Accounting Clerk Time (Hours/month)	3
Average # Invoices Mailed per Month	335
Postage per Invoice	$0.37
Total Average Invoice Processing Cost ($/month)	$184.52
Average Monthly Cost per 1000 Invoices	$550.81

Transit

LYNX assembled monthly costs for processing monthly and weekly passes for the period between November 2002 and March 2003. The average number of passes processed per month was used to calculate the average cost per pass processed. LYNX included in this cost:

- Salary/benefits cost for the customer service staff that sell the passes ($14.24 per hour times a number of hours per month used for pass sales, based on the actual number of passes sold and an assumed average transaction time of 30 seconds per pass sold);

- Cost of the passes themselves (at a cost of $0.11 per pass);

- Salary/benefit cost for the accounting clerks in the money room that process passes for distribution ($17.03 per hour times a number of hours used per month for pass processing); and

- Commissions for pass sales on consignment.

Table 12 summarizes this data. In addition, to presenting the basis for the costs in each reported month, we have also established the results for the entire period combined.

4.5 Quantitative Goal 9 – Characterize Current Processing Cost per Cash Transaction

ORANGES cards should have decreased cash processing costs for transit, parking and tolls. However, many types of cash processing savings will not be achieved until card use is more widespread. Thus, the limited use of smart cards in the test did not achieve significant cost savings in this area.

Table 12. Transit Pass Processing Costs

Month	# of Passes Sold	Cost for Customer Service Staff	Cost for Pass Stock	Cost for Money Room Staff	Cost for Consignment Sales Commissions	Total Cost	Cost per 1000 Passes Sold
November	7,282	$864.13	$793.74	$885,56	$2,087.85	$3,745.72	$514.38
December	5,986	$710.34	$652.47	$885.56	$2,105.90	$4,354.27	$727.41
January	8,034	$953.37	$875.71	$885.56	$2,890.30	$5,604.94	$697.65
February	7,935	$941.62	$864.92	$1,021.80	$2,240.20	$5,068.54	$638.76
March	9,064	$1,075.59	$987.98	$1,021.80	$2,195.04	$5,280.41	$582.57
Combined	38,301	$4,545.05	$4,174.82	$3,814.72	$11,519.29	$24,053.88	$628.02

However, characterizing current cash processing costs should indicate potential cost savings if bigger reductions in the use of cash were achieved through future full-scale deployment. The specific cost categories and assumptions included have been documented for use in any such future consideration of this data.

Measure

- Costs for processing cash, for each mode.

Data Collection and Analysis

Parking

The Parking Bureau assembled costs for the period from October 2002 through March 2003 related to the cash processing costs at each garage. The types of costs the Parking Bureau included were:

- A portion of the salary/benefits cost for the accounting clerk who counts the cash collected from garages, surface lots, and events.

The cash revenue processed during this period was used to calculate the average cost per dollar of cash processed. Table 13 summarizes this data for the three equipped garages and for all three garages combined, with costs and revenues being the totals for this 6-month period.

Table 13. Parking Garage Cash Processing Costs

Garage	Cash Processed	Cost for Money Counting Staff	Cost per $1000 Processed
Central Boulevard	$366,825	$2,002	$5.46
Market	$163,409	$2,002	$12.25
Library	$259,050	$2,002	$7.73
Combined	$789,284	$6,006	$7.61

Transit

LYNX assembled monthly costs for processing cash revenue for the period between November 2002 and March 2003. LYNX included in this cost:

- Salary/benefit cost for the accounting clerks in the money room who process cash revenue from both pass sales and fareboxes ($17.03 per hour times a number of hours used per month for cash processing); and

- Armored car charges to transport the pass sales cash from the sales location and farebox revenue from the garages to the money room location.

Table 14 summarizes this data. In addition to presenting the basis for the costs in each reported month, we have also established the combined results for the entire period.

Table 14. Transit Pass Processing Costs

Month	Cash Processed	Cost for Money Room Staff	Armored Car Charges	Total Cost	Cost per $1000 Cash Revenue
November	$929,890.90	$10,013.64	$1,966.89	$11,980.53	$12.88
December	$892,892.47	$10,013.64	$1,966.89	$11,980.53	$13.42
January	$987,955.97	$10,013.64	$1,838.89	$11,852.53	$12.00
February	$969,269.47	$9,877.40	$1,838.89	$11,716.29	$12.09
March	$936,840.97	$9,877.40	$1,882.96	$11,760.36	$12.55
Combined	$4,716,849.78	$49,795.72	$9,494.52	$59,290.24	$12.57

Tolls

OOCEA decided not to release cash processing costs data, so this goal could not be evaluated for this agency.

5   After Data Analysis for Quantitative Goals

5.1   Quantitative Goal 1 –Clearinghouse Performance Measures

The intent of this goal was to gather data for measures to characterize clearinghouse performance. This goal only applied to after testing.

Measures

- Transactions processed per hour

- Transaction processing error rate

- Timeliness of reporting and funds movement

Test Hypothesis

- The clearinghouse system will provide acceptable performance.

Data Collection and Analysis

- TranSend reported a total transaction volume during the demonstration of 197,403, broken down as follows:

    - Revenue transactions (ORANGES card transactions for payment or revaluing) – 14, 990 (in 9,661 batches[11])

    - Event transactions[12] – 63,947

    - Batch control records[13] – 118,556

- On this basis, TranSend estimated that, on average, 115 transactions were processed per hour. Based on the processing capabilities of the hardware, TranSend estimated the maximum capacity of the clearinghouse at roughly 180,000 transactions per hour.

---

[11] Transaction batches were sent to the clearinghouse hourly from the toll plaza and parking garages, daily from LYNX and at the end of each shift from revaluing terminals.

[12] Event transactions provide data on when specific user or system initiated events occur, to assist with monitoring system operation and troubleshooting.

[13] Batch control records were used to cross reference the contents of each batch and help prevent fraud.

- TranSend indicated that less than 1% of the transactions resulted in processing errors, due to missing, incomplete or duplicate transactions or log entry format errors[14]. TranSend also indicated that the most common causes for these errors included various aspects that likely could be addressed through improved agency equipment and training; these causes included:

  - Users withdrawing the card from the reader too quickly, referred to as a "torn" transaction

  - Agency device operator errors, such as incorrect dates configuration and duplicate transactions

  - Limitations of the agency devices, such as in the number of data elements supported per transaction, the card read range, error recovery capability and manual transaction collection procedures

- TranSend indicated that daily reports were provided the next day 100% of the time throughout the trial. TranSend also indicated that the bi-weekly funds movement instruction resulted in actual funds movement on the next day 90% of the time, and within two days 100% of the time.

5.2 Quantitative Goal 2 – Acceptance Test Results

The program manager provided results from acceptance testing completed as the system was brought into revenue service, to identify the degree to which the system met the functional requirements that were originally intended.

Measure

- Number of original system requirements achieved in the completed system.

Test Hypothesis

- The completed system will meet substantially all of the original requirements.

Data Collection and Analysis

- Initial testing used a prototype and pre-production "Pilot 1" version of the system in Orlando in early 2003.

- After pre-production testing of the "Pilot 2 Release 1" version of the software installed at TranSend (then known as TTI) offices in Phoenix, the software was installed on the

---

[14] Transactions associated with apparent software errors – discussed under the after data collection analysis for Goal7 - that inaccurately reports negative card balances, are not believed to be included in this figure.

system hardware in Orlando on August 3, 2003 and taken into its production phase (i.e., all cards used in the system after that date were tracked and reconciled using real money). This was also deemed the official start of the one-year demonstration period. Testing of the "Pilot 2 Release 1" version was completed on September 4, 2003.

- "Pilot 2 Release 2" incorporated several system capabilities, in particular: (1) automatic replenishment of toll accounts; (2) automatic renewal of monthly transit passes; and (3) the web-based customer interface. This version was tested in Phoenix and then installed in Orlando on December 16, 2003. Upon the completion of testing for "Pilot 2 Release 2", the ORANGES system was deemed fully operational in January 2004.

- Out of the 121 original system requirements, only 3 (detailed below) were not achieved by the fully operational ORANGES system. None of these were considered to have a critical impact on the ability of the system to function effectively as a demonstration. This is consistent with the test hypothesis that the completed system would meet all of the original requirements.

- The following were the specifics of the original system requirements that the agencies elected to waive in the completed system:

  - **Original:** The maximum electronic purse balance was to be $99, and the minimum load amount was to be $1.25.
    Accepted: The maximum electronic purse balance was $100, and any amount could be loaded.

  - **Original:** No minimum electronic purse balance was to be required for entering a parking garage.
    Accepted: Parking garage entry requires an electronic purse balance of at least $0.01.

  - **Original:** The toll lane reload device was to allow for payment from the toll account rather than the electronic purse, as a backup for the smart card accepting transponder equipment.
    Accepted: The toll lane reload device only allowed for payment from the electronic purse.

- It is not known whether these original system requirements were not achieved due to technical issues (e.g., equipment limitations, or insufficient time and/or resources for customization) or institutional issues (e.g., the requirement not being understood). It seems that the agencies decided to waive these requirements since there was a procedural alternative or a limited impact – and to allow TranSend to focus on addressing more critical issues needed to make the system ready for revenue service.

5.3 Quantitative Goal 3 – Demonstrate Performance for New Transponders

As of its use in this project, the EFKON smart card accepting transponder was unproven in North America; moreover, this device uses an infrared interface also unproven in North America. The goal for these new transponders was to demonstrate reliable equipment operation that would not interfere with customer reaction to the ORANGES card.

Measure

- Difference between the numbers of monthly transactions for smart card accepting and conventional transponders for vehicles equipped with both types passing the Holland East toll plaza.

Test Hypothesis

- For vehicles equipped with both types of transponder, the smart card accepting transponder will complete the same number of transactions passing through the Holland East toll plaza as the conventional transponder.

The EFKON equipment has been tested in Europe and Asia, but performance in the local environment needed to be established through the FOT. Vehicles equipped with the EFKON smart card accepting transponder were also equipped with a conventional transponder for use at other toll plazas. As a result, if both transponders were successfully read, two transactions were recorded when one of these vehicles passed through the Holland East toll plaza; OOCEA subsequently canceled the conventional transponder account transaction to avoid double charging. Significant operational problems with the smart card accepting transponder/reader equipment could therefore be detected through the recording of fewer smart card than conventional transponder transactions.

Data Collection and Analysis

During the six-month period from February 2004 through July 2004, the 16 customers whose vehicles were equipped with smart card accepting transponders completed a total of 813 EPASS transactions. During the same time period, however, only 530 transactions were completed with the EFKON transponders and reported to OOCEA through the ORANGES system. Hence, there was immediate cause for concern, as there appeared to be many cases where the EFKON transaction was not processed. The missing transactions could have resulted from (1) the EFKON transponder not being read, (2) the ORANGES smart card ID not being read, or (3) the transaction not being processed by the clearinghouse.

OOCEA reported anecdotal information suggesting that some of the customers provided with EFKON transponders did not mount them inside their windshields as requested, perhaps because it was to be only a one-year demonstration. Instead customers would hold up the transponder when passing through the lane, which may have interfered with the communications. Also, these customers in some cases may have forgotten to hold up the EFKON transponder altogether.

Three of the EFKON transponders were used throughout the demonstration period by OOCEA employees. These individuals are known to have properly mounted the transponders. In addition, one of the transponders was used by a PBS&J employee, but primarily during testing rather than throughout the demonstration period.

For the remaining 12 transponders, the large number of missed transactions for the EFKON transponders may have been a result of this potential improper mounting issue. In particular, no EFKON transactions were ever completed for 6 of the customer transponders. If any of these transponders were correctly mounted, there is no available information to explain why the transactions were not completed. Possible reasons include (1) the cardholder not knowing to insert the ORANGES card, (2) the cardholder knowing to insert the ORANGES card but choosing not to, (3) card damage, or (4) lack of transponder card reading capability. For this reason, the analysis focused only on the 3 transponders used by OOCEA staff, for which none of these issues were expected to have existed.

The following summarizes the specific findings for each of these 3 customers:

- For customer 3, there were 34 completed EFKON transactions and 41 completed EPASS transactions, indicating that for 17% of the transactions the EFKON lane reader was not able to complete the EKFON transponder ID reading transaction. The EFKON equipment completed no transactions for this customer in lane 6 -- but did complete transactions for this customer in other lanes -- during March-April 2004,, suggesting that during that period the EFKON reader equipment in that lane may have been faulty.

- For customer 4, there were 106 completed EFKON transactions and 113 completed EPASS transactions, indicating that for 6% of the transactions the EFKON lane reader was unable to complete the EKFON transponder ID reading transaction. For 67 of the completed EFKON transactions (including all transactions beginning May 17, 2004), the customer EFKON transponder ID was successfully read, while the smart card ID was not. As a result of the missing smart card ID information, the transactions were not processed by the ORANGES clearinghouse. Although there is no available information to identify the specific reason for the missing smart card ID information, possible reasons include (1) the smart card was not inserted into the transponder, or not inserted correctly, (2) the smart card was not operating correctly, or (3) the smart card reader in the transponder was not operating correctly.

- For customer 5, there were 30 completed EFKON transactions and 45 completed EPASS transactions, indicating that for 33% of the transactions the EFKON lane reader was unable to complete the EKFON transponder ID reading transaction. As with customer 3, the EFKON equipment completed no transactions for this customer in lane 6 -- but did complete transactions for this customer in other lanes – during March-April 2004, suggesting that during that period the EFKON reader equipment in that lane may have been faulty.

Thus, even with the 3 transponders that were presumed to have been correctly mounted, failure to read the transponder ID information was relatively common. In addition, there were several instances where successful EFKON transponder reads were unable to acquire the smart card ID information. Six transactions for these 3 customers were not successfully processed by the ORANGES clearinghouse <u>even though</u> both the transponder and smart card were read; the cause for this is not known. Moreover, there was no apparent pattern to these occurrences, in terms of a common time period, driver or plaza lane.

5.4   Quantitative Goal 4 – Reduce Transaction Times

Reducing average transaction times is important for all three modes and can translate directly into reduced queuing and bus dwell times. This quantitative goal was not applied to tolls for the evaluation, since the percentage of customers paying by transponder or smart card would not noticeably increase within the high volume of daily plaza transactions.

Measure

- Average payment transaction duration, for each mode and type of equipment.

Test Hypothesis

- Since prepaid payment transactions will be quicker than cash payment, the average payment transaction duration will decrease if the % prepaid increases.

Data Collection and Analysis

Parking

At each of the three equipped parking garages (Central Boulevard, Library and Market), a Parking Bureau observer recorded the duration for a sample of payment transactions at the cashier booth. The transaction time was taken as the amount of time the vehicle was stopped at the booth. Table 15 summarizes the sample size, average, standard deviation, and precision percentage for each of these samples. The confidence intervals on the averages for each garage were similar enough that it seemed reasonable to combine the garages together into a single large sample. For all garages together, it was possible to make the following statistical statement:

- Three garages combined: At the 95% confidence level, the average transaction time was expected to be 19.9 s +/- 6% (i.e., between 18.7 and 21.1 seconds, 95% of the time).

Table 15. Statistical Analysis of Parking Transaction Times Data

Garage	Sample Date	Sample Size	Average (s)	Standard Deviation (s)	Precision
Central Boulevard Garage	06/30	60	19.8	13.2	17%
	07/07	60	19.3	11.7	15%
	Combined	120	19.6	12.4	11%
Library Garage	06/22	62	16.7	11.1	17%
	07/22	62	18.8	9.4	12%
	Combined	124	17.8	10.3	10%
Market Garage	06/30	60	23.9	11.6	12%
	07/15	43	21.7	9.5	13%
	Combined	103	23.0	10.8	9%
All Garages Combined		347	19.9	11.4	6%

Transit

On buses for each of the two equipped LYNX routes (Links 13 and 15), the APC equipment was used to gather data during selected weeks when the buses were in use on these routes in May 2004 through July 2004 (only a subset of the LYNX bus fleet is APC-equipped). At each stop, the APC equipment recorded the number of passengers that boarded and alighted, as well as the duration of time the doors were open.

Several data filtering steps were taken to help construct samples where the duration the doors were open could be divided by the number of boarding passengers at that stop to best represent the average transaction time per boarding passenger at that stop:

- LYNX filtered out stop entries that were timepoints/layovers (either due to it being a known characteristic of the stop, excessive dwell time or having no passenger activity), or for some other reason might have involved the doors being open longer than needed for passenger movement alone.

- An additional filtering step by the evaluation team removed any remaining stop entries that involved at least 120 seconds per boarding passenger. It was assumed that these represented unrecognized delays beyond what was needed to board passengers (e.g., timepoints/layovers). This was a judgment in the sense that all longer durations per passenger (e.g., greater than about 30 seconds per passenger) might be of this type. On the other hand, some of these longer durations could be legitimately associated with a boarding passenger (e.g., trouble finding change or a fare dispute). Implicit in the test hypothesis was the expectation that the smart card would tend to reduce the incidence of longer fare payment events. Hence, retaining the somewhat longer duration stop entries in the samples (i.e., the longer ones that are less than 120 seconds) was intended to capture situations that may be mitigated by the smart card.

- The evaluation team noted that some stop entries seem infeasible (e.g., several people boarding within 1-2 seconds). This could indicate variations in the behavior of the APC equipment (e.g., over counting boardings, undercounting the duration of the door opening). There is no reason to believe that the underlying cause of these is limited only to these stop entries, and these have not been eliminated from the sample to avoid introducing a bias against short duration stop entries. It was assumed that these effects were prevalent to a similar degree in the before and after testing (i.e., so that they balance out in the before vs. after comparison).

- Passengers simultaneously board (through the front door) and alight (through the rear door). LYNX filtered out stop entries where the number of alighting passengers exceeded the number boarding, in which case the duration of the doors being open would not have been governed by the number of boarding passengers.

- An additional filtering step undertaken by the evaluation team was to remove stop entries listing a dwell time of zero, since these entries apparently represent faulty data.

Unfortunately, due to failures with the APC equipment, only the July data for Link 15 was successfully retrieved. LYNX reported that this occurred due to a combination of several hardware problems. Three of the LYNX fleet of APC-equipped buses had been equipped for ORANGES acceptance and designated for use as spare vehicles during the demonstration for Links 13 and 15. However, the wireless data transfer system had failed at some point during the after data collection period. This was only discovered when LYNX attempted to retrieve the June and July data from the buses in August 2004.

Once the wireless data system was repaired, retrieved data became available in September 2004 for review. After the timepoints and stops where alighting exceeded boardings were filtered out, little data remained. Upon investigation, it was discovered that each of these three vehicles had been out of service or had suffered an APC hardware failure[15] during the trial. Due to a delay in retrieving and analyzing the APC data, this remained undetected by LYNX until mid-September when the after data collection period had ended.

Table 16 summarizes the sample size, average, standard deviation, and precision percentage for this sample, for which it was possible to make the following statistical statement:

- Link 15: At the 95% confidence level, the average transaction time was expected to be 9.5 s +/- 6% (i.e., between 8.9 and 10.1 seconds, 95% of the time).

Table 16. Statistical Analysis of Transit Transaction Times Data

Bus Route	Sample Date	Sample Size	Average (s)	Standard Deviation (s)	Precision
Link 15	July	668	9.5	7.9	6%

5.5 Quantitative Goal 5 – Increase Prepaid Revenue Share

As suggested above, operating agencies generally wish to (1) reduce cash handling costs and (2) increase the "float" investment revenue earned from holding prepaid revenue. However, changes in cash handling costs and float revenue were not expected here due to the limited scale of the FOT test configuration. Prepaid revenue share was selected as a measurable surrogate quantitative goal for equipped facilities. It was therefore necessary to determine whether some of the ORANGES card usage was displaced from other prepaid payment methods rather than from cash. For this reason, we looked at the overall percentage using any prepaid method, rather than only the percentage using the ORANGES card. This goal was not applied to tolls for the evaluation, since the percentage paying by transponder would not noticeably increase within the high volume of daily plaza transactions.

Measure

- % of transactions that use a prepaid revenue payment method

---

[15] One vehicle had rear door sensor damage that damaged the vehicle's overall APC controller. Another had damage to the front door sensor only. Since passengers board through the front door, this rendered the data unusable for the purposes of the after data analysis. The third vehicle was out of service during most of the trial due to major maintenance unrelated to the APC equipment. LYNX is now discovering that their APC equipment has door sensors which are susceptible to inadvertent passenger damage due to their placement alongside the stairwells, and that they will need to retrieve data much more frequently to detect and repair such damage quickly.

Test Hypothesis

- % prepaid transactions will increase for equipment accepting the ORANGES card.

Data Collection and Analysis

Parking

The Parking Bureau was able to provide monthly summaries for each parking garage over the period from May 2004 through July 2004, indicating the amounts received for the following types of parking payment methods:

- Monthly parking permits – a prepaid method;

- Transient parking – cash payment at the exit cashier booth;

- Evening parking – cash payment on entry during the evening hours, so that the exit cashier booth can be unattended.

The prepaid revenue collected from the ORANGES transactions for each of these months was also available, but only in aggregated form for all three garages. The ORANGES revenue was allocated to the individual garages proportional to the distribution of non-ORANGES revenue. Table 17 presents this data (rounded to the nearest dollar). For each garage, the percent prepaid varies from month to month, so a statistical analysis was performed:

- Central Boulevard Garage: At the 95% confidence level, the average prepaid revenue share was expected to be 45% +/- 13% (i.e., between 39% and 51%, 95% of the time).

- Library Garage: At the 95% confidence level, the average prepaid revenue share was expected to be 38% +/- 8% (i.e., between 35% and 41%, 95% of the time).

- Market Garage: At the 95% confidence level, the average prepaid revenue share was expected to be 33% +/- 10% (i.e., between 30% and 37%, 95% of the time).

Table 17. Parking Prepaid Revenue Share Data

Garage	Month	Prepaid	ORANGES	Cash	Total	Prepaid + ORANGES Revenue Share
Central Boulevard	May	$59,004	$805	$56,995	$116,804	51%
	June	$44,811	$814	$64,898	$110,523	41%
	July	$37,895	$925	$51,027	$89,847	43%
Library	May	$26,416	$630	$48,426	$75,472	36%
	June	$31,595	$637	$55,090	$87,322	37%
	July	$35,555	$724	$52,947	$89,226	41%
Market	May	$15,386	$315	$27,153	$42,854	37%
	June	$13,565	$318	$30,043	$43,926	32%
	July	$12,065	$362	$27,344	$39,771	31%

Transit

LYNX was able to provide monthly summaries for the fareboxes on each route over the period from May 2004 through July 2004, indicating the percent of the ridership using the following categories of transit payment methods:

- Prepaid – passes, tickets and transfers – and free rides;
- Cash

Table 18 presents this data, which represents the prepaid share of the ridership, rather than the prepaid share of the revenue (i.e., the prepaid revenue share would be somewhat lower, given the lower average fare for prepaid riders). A statistical analysis was performed for the data beginning from May 2004:

- Link 13: At the 95% confidence level, the average prepaid ridership share was expected to be 67% +/- 1% (i.e., between 66% and 67%, 95% of the time).

- Link 15: At the 95% confidence level, the average prepaid ridership share was expected to be 62% +/- 2% (i.e., between 61% and 64%, 95% of the time).

Table 18. Transit Prepaid Ridership Share Data

Route	Month	Prepaid	ORANGES Pass	ORANGES Stored Value	Cash	Total	Prepaid + ORANGES Ridership Share
Link 13	May	23,495	69	12	11,894	35,470	66%
	June	24,315	90	3	12,074	36,482	67%
	July	23,062	56	5	11,202	34,325	67%
Link 15	May	28,073	75	9	17,669	45,826	61%
	June	27,611	102	5	15,924	43,642	64%
	July	27,057	77	5	16,778	43,917	62%

5.6 Quantitative Goal 6 – Increase Automated Payment Equipment Uptime

As indicated earlier, cash accepting equipment can suffer more downtime as the cash volume increases. This applies more to unattended automated devices than to attended locations, since these devices use mechanical devices to automate cash acceptance. By displacing cash use, the ORANGES card should have reduced downtime. This would reduce maintenance costs and revenue loss (i.e., at unattended devices where revenue cannot be collected while the device is down).

Measure

- % of operating hours with cash processing available (coins for toll ACMs; coins and bills for fareboxes)

Test Hypothesis

- The frequency and severity of planned and unplanned maintenance for unattended devices relates to the amount of cash processed. Cash processing availability should increase as % prepaid increases.

Data Collection and Analysis

Tolls

OOCEA was able to provide data on the times when the various lanes at the Holland East toll plaza were down due to a failure attributed to "ACM and tunnel vault" (see Table 19). ACM failures were expected to be a frequent occurrence in this category. This data was provided for the entire months from May 2004 through July 2004.

Only lanes 4 and 5 (westbound) and lanes 10 and 11 (eastbound) were equipped with ACMs. The percentage availability calculation was based on the fact that these four lanes operate continuously. For the purposes of the evaluation, combining the data for the 3-month period enhanced the overall value of the percentage availability measure.

The statistical assessment for this 3-month sample indicates:

- At the 95% confidence level, the average ACM % availability was expected to be 99.82% +/- 0.04% (i.e., between 99.78% and 99.85%, 95% of the time).

Table 19. Toll Lanes Automated Coin Machine Uptime Data

Month	Downtime (DD:HH:MM)	Availability
May	00:06:41	99.78%
June	00:04:30	99.84%
July	00:05:05	99.83%
Combined	00:16:16	99.82%

Transit

LYNX was able to provide data on the durations for which the farebox was not in service each day, for the ten fareboxes that were equipped for ORANGES acceptance for the period May 2004 through July 2004 (see Table 20). Combining this with the duration of service each day for the equipped vehicles allowed the farebox % availability to be calculated for each month. The specific cause of the various farebox downtime incidents was not available from this data, although it is generally known that problems with the cash accepting components and power supply were common causes of farebox incidents.

In this case, combining the data for the 3 months enhanced the overall value of the percentage availability measure. These durations have been combined for the ten fareboxes. The statistical assessment for this 3-month sample indicates:

- At the 95% confidence level, the average farebox % availability was expected to be 99.30% +/- 0.40% (i.e., between 98.90% and 99.70%, 95% of the time).

Table 20. Transit Farebox Uptime Data

Month	Scheduled for Operation (DD:HH:MM)	Operational (DD:HH:MM)	Availability
May	193:05:05	191:17:33	99.23%
June	191:12:14	189:13:34	98.98%
July	194:21:53	194:06:51	99.68%
Combined	579:15:12	575:13:58	99.30%

5.7 Quantitative Goal 7 – Joint Account Use

Agencies were interested in the degree to which the ORANGES cards would be used to travel using multiple modes and store high prepayments. This quantitative goal measured how and where cards were used, as opposed to other quantitative goals which were associated with the effects of card use.

Measures

- Cumulative probability distributions for transaction frequency, over the cardholder population, segregated between payment and revaluing transactions -- as well as by mode

- Cumulative probability distributions for transaction value, over the transaction population, segregated between payment and revaluing transactions -- as well as by mode

- Average stored value balance, for each card, segregated on the basis of card use frequency

- Percentage breakdown of the cardholder population, between cards used for one mode, for mode pairs or for all three modes

Test Hypothesis

- Most cardholders will maintain a prepaid balance and use the card regularly. Some may use the card alternately for transit and tolls (or transit and parking), some for downtown parking and toll payment.

Data Collection and Analysis

TranSend provided a sequence of weekly reports summarizing the ORANGES clearinghouse transactions. These weekly transaction reports supported various types of data analysis to examine how cardholders used the ORANGES system. The specific feasible measures and analyses based on the available clearinghouse transactions data varied somewhat from the measures projected in the original test plan (as discussed above). Since the full capabilities of the ORANGES system were in place as of January 2004, transactions data for the period from late January 2004 through the end of the demonstration (end of July 2004) was analyzed.

The agencies had adopted a target of maintaining 800-1200 active cards throughout the demonstration period[16]. Figure 6 summarizes the cumulative number of cards issued by the agencies over the course of the analysis period. From the initial card issuance in August 2003 through late January 2004, over 1000 cards were issued, and roughly 200 more cards were issued through June 2004.

However, the percentage of active cards (as shown in Figure 7) remained at roughly 10% through June 2004, and subsequently gradually declined to roughly 6% over the final month or so of the demonstration. This placed the number of active cards below 160 throughout the trial, which was well below the target. The decline in card use toward the end of the demonstration can be reasonably attributed to some degree to the fact that cardholders were reminded around this time that the demonstration was coming to an end after July 2004 – as well as to a normal summer decline in commuting activity.

Figure 6. Cumulative Cards Issued

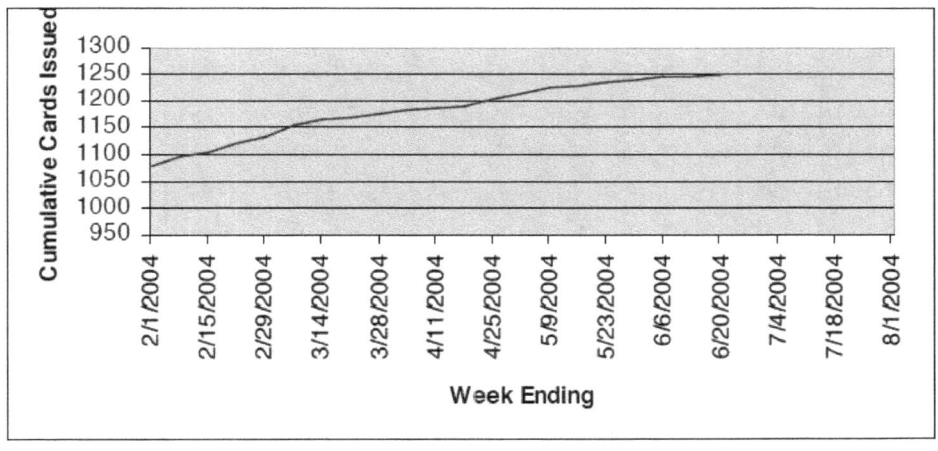

---

[16] A card became classified as active once first used, but subsequently classified as inactive if not used for three consecutive weeks.

Figure 7. Percentage Active Cards

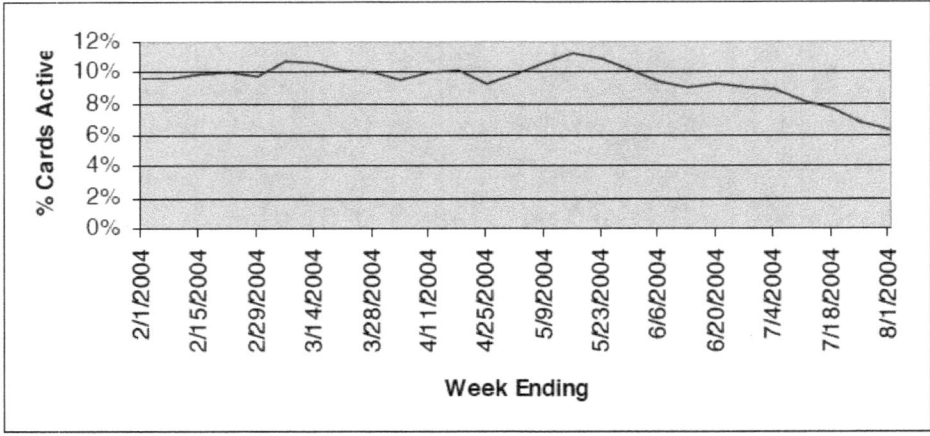

For each week, the numbers of active cardholders for various card use categories are summarized in Tables 21 and 22. Table 21 details the card use categories involving a single mode, while Table 22 addresses multimodal card use. The most common modal pattern of weekly card use was single mode use for parking, followed by single mode use for tolls. Over the course of the demonstration, multimodal card use for parking and tolls somewhat increased, but there was virtually no multimodal card use involving transit.

The evolution of the average card stored value balance over the February 2004 through July 2004 period is summarized in Figure 8. The trend was for the average stored value to decrease over the duration of the trial. In fact, if this graph is compared with the percentage active cards graph in Figure 7, we see that the shape is very similar. This suggests that the primary reason for the downwards shift in the average stored value balance was an increasing number of inactive cards carrying a small residual balance.

The stored value data shown in Figure 8 was calculated by averaging the average weekly card balances across all cardholders. Cards with a stored value balance of zero or $0.01 (parking cards were issued with this balance) were assumed to be inactive and excluded from the average. In a few cases where the stored value balance had been allowed to become negative, the balance was instead being reported as an extremely large positive balance. These false high balances were also excluded from the averages.

Table 21. Weekly Single Mode Cardholders

		# Payment Transactions								
	LYNX	0	0	0	0	0	0	1-5	6-9	10+
	OOCEA	0	0	0	1-5	6-9	10+	0	0	0
	Parking	1-5	6-9	10+	0	0	0	0	0	0
Week Ending	2/1/04	7	-	-	12	2	1	2	-	-
	2/8/04	9	-	-	7	4	1	1	1	1
	2/15/04	11	-	-	9	2	-	-	-	2
	2/22/04	14	1	-	8	2	-	1	-	1
	2/29/04	17	-	-	6	2	-	-	2	-
	3/7/04	22	-	-	7	3	1	1	-	-
	3/14/04	22	-	-	7	3	1	1	-	-
	3/21/04	20	4	-	5	2	-	-	-	1
	3/28/04	26	1	-	6	2	-	2	-	1
	4/4/04	15	-	-	4	2	-	-	-	1
	4/11/04	24	4	-	3	2	-	-	-	1
	4/18/04	29	5	-	6	-	1	-	-	1
	4/25/04	27	4	1	7	-	1	3	1	-
	5/2/04	30	4	2	5	-	-	3	-	-
	5/9/04	40	1	-	6	-	-	3	-	-
	5/16/04	37	4	-	3	-	1	2	-	1
	5/23/04	33	7	-	5	-	-	1	-	-
	5/30/04	33	4	-	3	-	-	-	1	-
	6/6/04	36	1	-	4	-	-	1	1	-
	6/13/04	33	3	-	2	1	-	1	-	-
	6/20/04	35	2	1	3	1	-	-	2	-
	6/27/04	31	8	1	-	-	-	1	1	-
	7/4/04	35	6	1	1	-	-	2	-	1
	7/11/04	27	-	-	4	-	-	2	-	-
	7/18/04	31	2	-	1	-	-	2	-	1
	7/25/04	21	1	-	2	-	-	1	-	-
	8/1/04	25	1	-	2	-	-	-	-	-

Table 22. Weekly Multiple Mode Cardholders

	# Payment Transactions				
LYNX	0	0	0	0	1-5
OOCEA	1-5	1-5	6-9	10+	1-5
Parking	1-5	6-9	1-5	1-5	1-5
2/1/04	-	-	-	-	-
2/8/04	-	-	-	-	-
2/15/04	-	-	-	1	-
2/22/04	-	-	-	-	1
2/29/04	-	-	-	-	-
3/7/04	-	1	1	-	-
3/14/04	-	1	1	-	-
3/21/04	1	-	-	-	-
3/28/04	-	-	-	-	-
4/4/04	1	-	-	-	-
4/11/04	-	-	-	-	-
4/18/04	2	-	-	1	-
4/25/04	1	-	-	1	-
5/2/04	-	-	-	1	-
5/9/04	1	1	1	1	-
5/16/04	3	1	1	-	-
5/23/04	1	-	-	1	-
5/30/04	4	-	-	-	-
6/6/04	-	-	-	-	-
6/13/04	4	-	-	-	-
6/20/04	2	-	1	-	-
6/27/04	4	1	-	-	-
7/4/04	1	1	-	-	-
7/11/04	2	-	-	-	-
7/18/04	3	-	-	-	-
7/25/04	3	-	-	-	-
8/1/04	-	-	-	-	-

(Left axis label: Week Ending)

This inaccurate balance issue was not noticed by the clearinghouse or the agencies during the demonstration, and by the end of the demonstration affected five cards. In each case, the problem originated when the card was used for a transaction amount greater than the remaining balance (e.g., a $3 payment against a $1 balance). Rather than correctly reporting a negative balance, the system would instead indicate a value approaching $43 million. A subsequent revalue transaction was observed to correctly restore a positive balance (e.g., a $3 payment against a $1 balance, followed by a $10 revalue would correctly show a $8 balance), and subsequent payments would reduce the very large balance by the correct amount.

This had two practical effects: (1) during the trial the five cardholders in question (who may or may not have noticed) continued to successfully use the card for payments while the card accumulated a successively larger negative balance (although it was not being recorded as negative); and (2) the false balances were first noticed when the balance was checked for the purpose of providing the card refund at the end of the trial.

TranSend, after investigating this issue once they became aware of it at the end of the FOT, indicated that the clearinghouse was not configured to perform any checks for negative balance or over balance conditions (the maximum allowable stored value balance for the FOT was to be $100). Their understanding had been that the card or card reader was responsible to check for and disallow transactions that would result in a negative balance condition. Apparently, if the card was asked to debit an amount larger than the stored value balance, the result was the undesirable "roll under" effect that was observed. Neither the card nor the card reader were apparently configured with the logic to prevent this, and the clearinghouse was not configured with the logic to detect/report it to the agencies.

Figure 8. Average Stored Value Balance

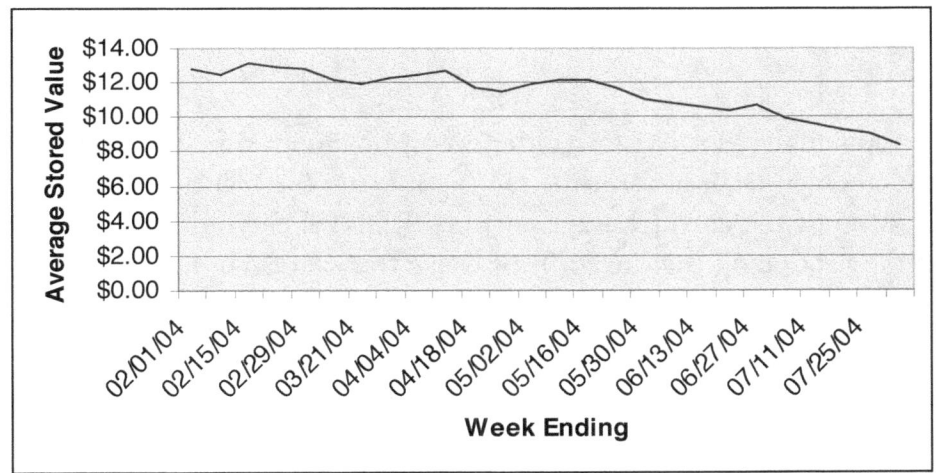

6 Comparison of Before and After Quantitative Data

This section compares the statistical analysis results for those quantitative goals for which there was both before and after testing. In addition, this section presents conclusions based on these comparisons that seem reasonable.

Note that, if the 95% confidence intervals for the before and after data do not overlap, this was interpreted as providing evidence supporting a statistically significant change. Where the confidence intervals do overlap, larger samples might have resulted in evidence supporting a statistically significant change (i.e., through establishing narrower confidence intervals that eliminate the overlap).

6.1 Quantitative Goal 4 – Reduce Transaction Times

Parking

The before testing statistical analysis concluded:

- Three garages combined: At the 95% confidence level, the average transaction time was expected to be 23.3 s +/- 5% (i.e., between 22.1 and 24.5 seconds, 95% of the time).

The after testing statistical analysis concluded:

- Three garages combined: At the 95% confidence level, the average transaction time was expected to be 19.9 s +/- 6% (i.e., between 18.7 and 21.1 seconds, 95% of the time).

Comparing the two analyses provides evidence supporting a statistically significant reduction in the average transaction time. This supports the test hypothesis that the conversion of some of the cash transactions to ORANGES would reduce the average transaction time by reducing the duration of these transactions.

As discussed under Goal 5, a drop in the use of monthly permits between the before and after periods resulted in the after period having a greater cash share. This strengthens the significance of the reduced average transaction time, since the expected effect would have been an increase in average transaction time.

Transit

The before testing statistical analysis concluded:

- Link 13: At the 95% confidence level, the average transaction time was expected to be 13.0 s +/- 4% (i.e., between 12.5 and 13.5 seconds, 95% of the time).

- Link 15: At the 95% confidence level, the average transaction time was expected to be 10.6 s +/- 3% (i.e., between 10.3 and 10.9 seconds, 95% of the time).

The after testing statistical analysis concluded:

- Link 15: At the 95% confidence level, the average transaction time was expected to be 9.5 s +/- 6% (i.e., between 8.9 and 10.1 seconds, 95% of the time).

A before and after comparison was undertaken only for Link 15, as a result of the limited availability of after data due to the LYNX APC equipment failures. With less data in the Link 15 after sample than the Link 15 before sample, the Link 15 after data confidence interval is substantially wider than the Link 15 before data confidence interval. Nonetheless, comparing the two Link 15 analyses provides evidence supporting a statistically significant reduction in the average transaction time. This supports the test hypothesis that the conversion of some of the cash transactions to ORANGES would reduce the average transaction time by reducing the duration of these transactions.

As discussed under Goal 5, however, there were few ORANGES transactions, as well as an overall shift from cash to period passes between the before and after data. This suggests that the observed reduction in average transaction time is more attributable to the increased pass use than to the ORANGES transactions.

6.2 Quantitative Goal 5 – Increase Prepaid Revenue Share

Parking

The before testing statistical analysis concluded:

- Central Boulevard Garage: At the 95% confidence level, the average prepaid revenue share was expected to be 52% +/- 12% (i.e., between 45% and 58%, 95% of the time).

- Library Garage: At the 95% confidence level, the average prepaid revenue share was expected to be 46% +/- 16% (i.e., between 39% and 53%, 95% of the time).

- Market Garage: At the 95% confidence level, the average prepaid revenue share was expected to be 47% +/- 14% (i.e., between 40% and 54%, 95% of the time).

The after testing statistical analysis concluded:

- Central Boulevard Garage: At the 95% confidence level, the average prepaid revenue share was expected to be 45% +/- 13% (i.e., between 39% and 51%, 95% of the time).

- Library Garage: At the 95% confidence level, the average prepaid revenue share was expected to be 38% +/- 8% (i.e., between 35% and 41%, 95% of the time).

- Market Garage: At the 95% confidence level, the average prepaid revenue share was expected to be 33% +/- 10% (i.e., between 30% and 37%, 95% of the time).

Comparing the two analyses for each of the garages does not provide evidence supporting a statistically significant change in the prepaid revenue share for the Central and Library garages, but does provide evidence supporting a statistically significant decrease in the prepaid revenue share for the Market garage.

The before data spans the October 2002 through March 2003 time period, and the after data spans the June 2004 through August 2004 time period. The before and after data in Tables 7 and 17 indicate a drop in both overall and monthly permit parking revenue during the summer after period, which may result from reduced parking use by commuters (who are most likely to use a monthly permit) during summer vacation periods.

Given the longer transaction times for cash relative to prepaid transactions, the observed similar or higher share for cash transactions in the after period, all things being equal, should have tended to increase the average parking transaction time. This serves to strengthen the importance of the observed decrease in average parking transaction time under Goal 4, suggesting an even greater reduced transaction time effect for the ORANGES card transactions.

Transit

The before testing statistical analysis concluded:

- Link 13: At the 95% confidence level, the average prepaid ridership share was expected to be 58% +/- 3% (i.e., between 57% and 60%, 95% of the time).

- Link 15: At the 95% confidence level, the average prepaid ridership share was expected to be 57% +/- 2% (i.e., between 56% and 58%, 95% of the time).

The after testing statistical analysis concluded:

- Link 13: At the 95% confidence level, the average prepaid ridership share was expected to be 67% +/- 1% (i.e., between 66% and 67%, 95% of the time).

- Link 15: At the 95% confidence level, the average prepaid ridership share was expected to be 62% +/- 2% (i.e., between 61% and 64%, 95% of the time).

Comparing the two analyses for each of the routes provides evidence supporting a statistically significant increase in the prepaid ridership share. Examining the before and after data in Tables 10 and 20 reveals that there were few ORANGES transactions, but a clear shift from cash to prepaid passes between the two time periods. This suggests that the reduced average transaction time discussed under Goal 4 is more attributable to the increase in pass use than to the ORANGES transactions.

6.3 Quantitative Goal 6 – Increase Automated Payment Equipment Uptime

Tolls

The before testing statistical analysis concluded:

- At the 95% confidence level, the average ACM % availability was expected to be 99.38% +/- 0.37% (i.e., between 99.02% and 99.74%, 95% of the time).

The after testing statistical analysis concluded:

- At the 95% confidence level, the average ACM % availability was expected to be 99.82% +/- 0.04% (i.e., between 99.78% and 99.85%, 95% of the time).

Comparing the two analyses provides evidence supporting a statistically significant increase in the ACM % availability. This supports the test hypothesis that introducing the ORANGES transactions reduced the usage of the ACM equipment by reducing the number of cash transactions. Since none of the ORANGES cardholders were previously an EPASS transponder user, the ORANGES transactions were expected to have been diverted from former cash transactions.

Transit

The before testing statistical analysis concluded:

- At the 95% confidence level, the average farebox % availability was expected to be 99.12% +/- 0.19% (i.e., between 98.93% and 99.31%, 95% of the time).

The after testing statistical analysis concluded:

- At the 95% confidence level, the average farebox % availability was expected to be 99.30% +/- 0.40% (i.e., between 98.90% and 99.70%, 95% of the time).

Comparing the two analyses does not provide evidence supporting a statistically significant change in the average farebox % availability. For Goal 5, it was concluded that there was an increase in the prepaid revenue share (attributable primarily to a shift from cash to period passes), which, all things being equal, would have been expected to improve the farebox % availability by decreasing the number of cash transactions.

7   Discussion Group Process

7.1 *Overview and Organization*

The Evaluation Test Plans document identified the data collection requirements for the set of goals and measures established in collaboration with the Implementation Team. As part of this data collection effort, qualitative data was collected via three discussion groups. Each discussion groups was comprised of 10-15 individuals. The discussion groups represented: (1) customers and cardholders; (2) operations and maintenance staff; and (3) management and planning staff. The purpose of the discussion groups was to elicit information, opinions and preferences regarding the use of the ORANGES smart card.

The Implementation Team managed the logistics for conducting these discussion groups (i.e., facility, refreshments, incentive payment). However, the federal Evaluation Team also played a direct role in helping with these arrangements, to help ensure that its goals would be met. The discussion groups were conducted at a meeting room at OOCEA. This facility was selected: (1) to allow for providing understandable directions to attendees; (2) to allow for evening access, given the location and building security; (3) to provide adequate visitor parking nearby; (4) to provide for access using the equipped LYNX Links 13 and 15; (5) because it offered sufficient space; and (6) to provide washroom facilities.

Each group had a facilitator from the Evaluation Team to guide the discussion. The discussion group facilitator elicited responses from group participants using open-ended style questions and polling. Discussion groups focused on and collected information about the following general topics:

- Cardholders
  - General benefits
  - Ease of use
  - Convenience of revaluing
- Operations and maintenance staff
  - General benefits
  - Reduced payment disputes
  - Reduced transfer abuse
  - Ease of customer use
  - Ease of operator use

- Maintenance

- Training

- Planning and management staff

  - General benefits

  - More comprehensive data collection

7.2 Selection of Discussion Group Members

Discussion group participant selection involved a collaborative effort by the Implementation Team and the federal Evaluation Team.

General Selection Criteria

Recruited customers (cardholders) represented the three smart card uses (transit, tolls and parking):

- **For toll customers**, the primary selection criterion was a regular travel pattern that involves the toll plaza included in the test (i.e., Holland).

- **For parking customers**, the primary criterion was regular use of one of three downtown parking garages included in the test (i.e., CBG, Library or Market).

- **For transit customers**, the primary criterion was regular ridership on Links (routes) included in the test (i.e., Link 13 or 15). There was also an attempt to include cardholders who used facilities from two or more of the agencies.

Pre-screening Criteria for Cardholders

Each of the three implementing agencies took responsibility for recruiting a number of cardholders. As part of this effort, the Implementation Team gathered pre-screening information to assist with selecting discussion group participants. Appendix B includes the discussion group pre-screening questions used during the LYNX recruitment effort.

The Evaluation Team reviewed cardholder characteristics as gathered by the implementing agencies through the recruitment efforts, and clustered them into recruitment subgroups (e.g., recruit 5 from toll users, 5 from LYNX Link 13 and 15 riders, and 5 from parking customers.). The Implementation Team used these subgroups to recruit cardholder discussion group participants, using phone, mail or email to solicit potential participation.

Employee Selection Process

These participants were selected by the agencies prior to FOT implementation. The Evaluation Team recommended (1) that the agencies avoid relying entirely on voluntary participation, and (2) that the agencies ensure that participating employees would be separated from their supervisors; it was felt that there would be a benefit to having both those who wish to speak and those more reluctant to speak involved in this process. The agencies submitted their sets of selected employee participants to the Evaluation Team in advance, to assist in preparing for the discussion groups.

7.3 Discussion Group Conduct

The FOT included the conduct of facilitated and focused discussion groups before the operational test period, as well as near the end of the demonstration period (i.e., for after testing). The before test sessions were held shortly after the start of the initial pilot FOT. The after sessions were held within a month after the completion of the FOT.

The discussion groups each lasted about two hours and were conducted in a comfortable setting. This provided adequate time for dialogue among the participants and the facilitator (from TranSystems) in response to a set of open-ended questions. The Implementation Team identified an appropriate venue for the sessions (i.e., a conference room at OOCEA headquarters), with assistance from the Evaluation Team.

The general approach to the discussions were to combine open-ended questions with "polling" type questions where the participants were asked to choose or rank from several presented or group-generated options. The general role of the facilitator was simply to ensure that the discussion kept moving, as well as to ensure that certain participants did not disproportionately dominate the discussion. One of the challenges with the groups was to avoid having too much time consumed with generalized complaints that were unrelated to the operational test. This was done in a way that recognized that allowing a limited amount of such "venting" can contribute to the participants' general openness in responding to the questions.

Cardholder Group

Recruited cardholders were taken through a structured group discussion that drew out their perceptions about key aspects of the program. The cardholder discussion group focused on matters involving the following:

- Convenience of use

- Trust and comfort level of use

- Reporting and informational needs (statements, etc.)

- Discounts and incentives

- Attitudinal perceptions regarding investment of effort by the agencies - as compared with focusing on core functions (e.g., does a multipurpose smart card have benefits to users and is this a worthwhile effort of the agencies?)

The Implementation Team provided a stipend of $50 to each customer group/cardholder participant.

Employee Groups

Employee groups included representatives from the transit, tolls and parking agencies. The employee information collected included:

- Gender and age (within set age ranges)

- Employer

- Employee work function (planning, management, operations or maintenance category, and their specific role in the organization)

Employee discussion groups focused on matters involving the following:

- Perceived convenience of use to customers

- Convenience of use to the agency

- Perceived trust and comfort level of use by customer

- Trust and comfort level of use by the employee (e.g., are there concerns that employers will be monitoring employees, for example?)

- Trust and comfort level of use by the agency (e.g., are there management concerns such as privacy, liability, monitoring employees, etc.?)

- Reporting and informational needs (data collection, reports, statements, data storage, record-keeping, market research, marketing, etc.)

- Discounts and incentives (planning, management, marketing, record-keeping)

- Reliability and quality control (operations, maintenance, planning, management issues)

- Attitudinal perceptions regarding investment of effort by agency as compared with focusing on core functions (e.g., does a multipurpose smart card have benefits to users and is this a worthwhile effort of the agencies?)

7.4 Discussion Group Scripts

The conduct of the discussion groups followed a series of open-ended questions and group polling to elicit views, opinions, attitudes and suggestions about the FOT. Although the discussion group scripts directed the facilitator in leading the discussion groups, they were not intended to be followed verbatim but were rather used as a map for the facilitator. The facilitator used his discretion to follow relevant discussion trails as they became clear.

The cardholder group participants were instructed to arrive 15 minutes prior to the start of the discussion group to assure that the session started on time. The employee group participants were instructed to arrive a few minutes prior to the scheduled session start and sign in, noting their name, organization, and position. For both types of groups, participants were then invited to enter the venue and have a seat as they completed the sign-in process. Refreshments were available and participants were invited to partake. Once the group was present, the facilitator introduced himself and stated his role. As explained above, this role was to ask questions of the group, facilitate expression of opinions, record ideas on a flipchart and ensure that everyone had a chance to speak.

8 Comparison of Before and After Discussion Group Findings

The before and after discussion group findings are compared below. Appendix B provides a more detailed summary of the questions and responses.

8.1 Cardholders Groups

Cardholders were asked about transportation conditions in Central Florida. Transportation conditions in Central Florida continued to be viewed as challenging, and mobility as inadequate.

Cardholders were asked for ideas for how mobility within the region can be improved. Cardholders seemed to be looking to transit options to improve regional transportation conditions.

Cardholders were asked if transportation conditions had improved since the first session (before test). Cardholders reported that the boarding and fare payment process for the bus service was improved with the ORANGES card, being faster and more convenient, with no need to worry about having exact change for the correct fare. This was true for tolls and parking as well. This perception of customer convenience seemed to be related to the "no hassle" benefit of electronic fare payment. This seemed to directly support the stated increased propensity to use the tollway, a parking garage or a bus route as a result of having the ORANGES card.

Cardholders were asked if they would be more or less likely to use a method of transportation other than their usual one if the form of payment was not a factor. Increased use of multiple modes apparently was not a significant byproduct of the card. Some cardholders indicated using their usual travel modes more often, though, because having the card eliminated instances when they might previously have not had cash available for the fare, toll or parking fee. Convenience and avoiding the need to pay at the point of purchase also seemed to be strong cardholder motivators.

Cardholders were asked if developing a common payment system for tolls, transit fares and city parking garages made sense, and if this made sense today and in the future. In the before group, the response was affirmative in all cases. Developing a common payment system for tolls, fares and parking fees was seen to make sense today and in the future, since it would make these services work better together and provide customer convenience. The cardholders echoed this view in the after test group, agreeing that a common payment method made sense today and in the future and made travel more convenient.

Cardholders were asked how the ORANGES card would and did affect them.
Cardholders universally stated in the before test that the card would provide convenience.
In the after test they universally stated that the card provided convenience -- and in fact
improved the transportation experience.

**Cardholders were asked about the concept and then the experience of revaluing the
ORANGES card.** Before the test, cardholders expressed interest in revaluing the card
online and at third party locations. After the test, cardholders expressed disappointment at
the limited options for replenishing value.

**Cardholders were asked if they would pay a nominal fee or deposit when the card is
issued or replaced.** Cardholders were consistent on this issue. Cardholders thought the
initial card should be free, but that it was fair to require a nominal fee of up to $10 if a lost
or stolen card had to be replaced.

Cardholders were asked about incentives. Cardholders remained consistent about
incentives, viewing them favorably and feeling that they should be based on usage (i.e., the
more you use the card, the greater the discount).

Cardholders were asked about their comfort level with using the ORANGES card.
During the before test session, concerns were generally about liabilities and risks associated
with the card. The general comfort level before using the card was 7.6 out of 10, on a scale
of 1 (very uncomfortable) to 10 (very comfortable). After the test, the general comfort
level increased to 9.3.

**Cardholders were asked about the ability to access their account and use
information.** The cardholders in the before test session wanted the ability to access date,
time, location and amount of all transactions. They wanted this access at any time online
or by phone and to receive a monthly statement. After the test, although all cardholders
felt that their account and personal information was safe, some stated that they had found
discrepancies in their account statements.

**Cardholders were asked their views about the need for and value of developing
smart card applications.** Cardholders completely supported the need for and value of
local and federal transportation agencies exploring smart card applications. This attitude
was strengthened through the test. Cardholders expressed that they would have been
disappointed if there was unwillingness on the part of the local agencies to develop ways to
use technology to make services more convenient and more secure.

Cardholders were asked for comments and suggestions after their experience with the ORANGES project. Cardholders suggested that smart card applications be made available nationwide, so that one card could be used to travel all over the US, with an emphasis on making the card compatible with other systems, services, and markets.

8.2 Planning and Management Staff

The P&M Staff group was asked which transportation issues were important to them. P&M Staff before and after test responses were consistent. Improving and maintaining travel speed is important for all modes, as are safety, convenience, and efficiency. Making service more widely available, in terms of service coverage and service frequency, was important to LYNX. Controlling costs was also cited as important.

The P&M Staff group was asked how well existing transportation investments match transportation needs and for suggestions to improve mobility. P&M Staff in the before session responded largely from the perspective of their respective agencies. In the after test, the responses more reflected an integrated and regional transportation perspective.

The P&M Staff group was asked about their views on the need for and value of developing smart card applications. P&M Staff in the before session expressed positive views about the need for a common fare payment system and its potential to lower overhead costs, indicating that this makes sense in the long run and might even make sense today. In the after session, the perspectives expressed were more focused on the limited extent of the test. The overarching view was that it makes sense to have the option for common fare payment but that existing payment options will need to be retained as well.

The P&M Staff group was asked about providing customer convenience. P&M Staff views on customer convenience did not change. They recognized the potential of the ORANGES card to improve customer convenience.

The P&M Staff group was asked about the relevance of this test to their agencies, agency employees and to them personally. P&M Staff views shifted from an agency to a regional perspective. In terms of the potential impact of the test on the agency, the concerns in the before session were primarily technical in focus. Responses in the after session were more general while remaining technical in focus. In the before session the employees identified some personal potential for opportunity as well as some risk from being involved in the test. In the after session however, these perspectives were much more positive.

The P&M Staff group was asked about potential trust issues. P&M Staff were asked their views of potential trust issues for their agencies and customers, as well as their views from an employee perspective. The perceived customer comfort level rose from an average score of 5.7 out of 10 before the test to an average 7.0 out of 10 after the test (the customer comfort level indicated by the cardholders discussion group was 9.3). In the after session, staff noted that concerns going into the test were generally no longer concerns by the end. The agencies and employees felt that they had established enough trust in each other to work together, especially through resolving problems that surfaced with the system.

The P&M Staff group was asked about equipment reliability. P&M Staff had concerns going into the test about the reliability of the equipment and the overall system. These concerns continued through the test, although they were reduced over time. There were more staff issues than expected (mostly with LYNX), because so many personnel were involved in the process from one day to the next. Inadequate training was a key issue.

The P&M Staff group was asked about planning and management issues. P&M Staff had concerns prior to the test that centered on coordination, marketing and logistics. In the after test session, staff was much more focused on overcoming inherent shortcomings in the test, indicating that with a larger travel market and a more extensive and integrated transportation system (i.e., adding rail and park-and-rides to tolls, parking and buses), the impact of the card would be greater than with the limited size and scope of the FOT test configuration.

The P&M Staff group was asked about information, record keeping and accuracy. P&M Staff had concerns in the before session that centered on data integrity, system reliability, and system support. In the after session, staff considered the data to have been reliable, but focused on problems and shortcomings they encountered during the test.

The P&M Staff group was asked about incentives. P&M Staff thought that the test was a great opportunity to partner with other agencies and offer attractive incentives to customers. In the after test session, staff cited a difficulty in getting agency approvals for incentives. Staff agreed that in a full-scale deployment, incentives should be based on usage.

The P&M Staff group was asked about the relevance of and the need to examine smart card applications. P&M Staff in the before session agreed that it was relevant and important to explore the use of smart cards. These views did not change in the after session. Staff felt that while the ORANGES system demonstration was a worthwhile investment, the timing may not be right for full-scale deployment of this application in Central Florida (i.e., until the market reaches some greater critical mass that would make this type of system cost-effective).

The P&M Staff group was asked for comments and suggestions following participation in the ORANGES test. P&M Staff suggested that agencies keep an open mind about future applications and look for future partnering opportunities with other agencies. Overall, the P&M Staff participants were positive and pragmatic about this test, indicating that they had learned valuable lessons.

8.3   Operations and Maintenance Staff

The O&M Staff group was asked about transportation issues important to them. At the O&M Staff level, the perception of important transportation issues broadened over the course of the test to include elements outside this group's normal scope. O&M Staff were also asked about current transportation investments. The after test session responses were concerned more with broader issues.

The O&M Staff group was asked about the value of developing smart card applications. O&M Staff responded in the before session with a positive view about developing smart card applications today and in the future. In the after session, the views did not change much. The group felt that a common payment system would work better in the future when demand was greater and the transit system more extensive.

The O&M Staff group was asked about providing customer convenience. O&M Staff responses were positive in both the before and after test sessions. This group continued to recognize the value of providing customer convenience.

The O&M Staff group was asked their views about the relevance of the test to the mission of the agencies. Overall, the group was positive about the test and its relevance to the mission of each agency. The O&M staff group's before session responses were generally positive, but often specific and focused on the potential for failure. The O&M staff after session view of the test again was generally positive, but again the comments and concerns often focused on specifics.

The O&M Staff group was asked their views concerning trust issues. This group felt that the customer comfort level was high throughout the test. As agency employees, the group had concerns in the after session involving transitioning the reconciliation and error handling procedures from the test to a full-scale operation.

The O&M Staff group was asked their views concerning equipment reliability. O&M Staff responses were consistent in before and after test sessions, with the after test session including many suggestions for mitigating problems encountered through the test.

The O&M Staff group was asked their views concerning the need to explore use of smart cards. O&M Staff responses in the before test session and the after test session were consistent, being in favor of exploring and developing smart card technology applications today and for the future.

The O&M Staff group was asked for comments and suggestions following the ORANGES test. O&M Staff indicated that the system should focus on ensuring a user-friendly and well-integrated system for agency personnel and for the customer.

9   Assessment of Key Issues and Lessons Learned

This section reviews key issues and lessons learned from the ORANGES demonstration. The issues and lessons are documented in greater detail in thee minutes from the monthly evaluation conference calls, which have been included as Appendix C.

9.1   Key Issues

The original premise of the ORANGES FOT was that it would demonstrate the institutional and technical issues associated with multiple agencies using a single smart card and common stored value purse to pay for transit, tolls and parking in Orlando. As anticipated, several notable issues emerged during the course of the project:

- **Changes in the Details of the FOT Test Configuration:** There have been several changes in the types of smart card use that ORANGES FOT would support:

  - **Transit:**

    - *Smart card and reader:* LYNX originally intended to purchase new GFI Odyssey validating fareboxes equipped to accept a smart card. A dual interface card (with contactless and contact interfaces) was preferred, to facilitate use with parking meters, parking payment kiosks and certain types of card balance revaluing equipment. However, in late 2001 GFI was only offering integrated smart card readers for the Odyssey farebox from Sony and Cubic. The proprietary smart cards that work with these readers were not available in dual interface versions at the time of the FOT. A reader was desired that would use the ISO standard Type A or Type B contactless interface, for which dual interface smart cards were commercially available at the time of the FOT. Although the Cubic Tri-Reader can currently support Type A, Type B and Cubic proprietary card technology, the GFI implementation of this reader on its fareboxes as of late 2001 did not yet support the Type A or B cards. The development of support for the Type A card needed for ORANGES was scheduled, but would not have been available to the project until sometime in 2003 and this would have caused an implementation delay.

    Transit-toll systems integration issues: By early 2002, LYNX was leaning towards adopting the Sony card and reader type offered by GFI and accepting the limitations associated with using a contactless-only smart card. However, the decision to adopt EFKON equipment for the toll plaza implementation required use of the Mifare contactless interface for compatibility[17]. EFKON was willing to

---

[17] Mifare is a variant on the Type A interface, available from several card manufacturers.

provide its existing hardware and software to the project, and the EFKON equipment supported Mifare technology but not the Sony card. A dual interface smart card with a Mifare contactless interface was selected from Gemplus, but this meant that an external "stand-alone" smart card reader was needed for LYNX. "Proxibus" readers from Ascom were selected for LYNX buses.

One important implication of this stand-alone validator approach was the resulting absence of a driver interface (i.e., validator keypad and display). LYNX chose not to install an additional driver interface.[18] This resulted in certain associated limitations in passenger options. For example, if allowed by the card reader logic, an interface could have permitted the driver to collect the fare for an accompanying person from stored value on the same card after a passenger had paid his/her fare with a period pass.

- ## Tolls:

  - OOCEA was initially reluctant to integrate smart card accepting transponders or laneside smart card readers with its existing transponder-based toll collection system. OOCEA expressed a concern with potential integration costs and temporary disruptions to the operation of the existing system during integration. There was also an initial reluctance to equip the system with laneside smart card readers, based on an underlying concern about whether this might negatively affect transponder market penetration of EPASS.

  In early 2002, EFKON was selected to provide a system for smart card accepting transponders that would operate in a manner almost entirely independent from the existing toll system. These transponders and readers use infrared technology for short-range communications. The integration was limited to a signal from the EFKON equipment to activate the laneside displays (traffic lights) that tell drivers when the toll has been collected so that they can proceed through the plaza. In October 2002, OOCEA decided to also incorporate the EFKON "Touch'N'Go" laneside readers in selected lanes.

- ## Parking:

  - The City of Orlando Parking Bureau initially planned to accept the smart card at garage entrance and exit lanes, parking meters and parking payment kiosks. In 2001, a decision was made to not incorporate smart card readers into parking kiosks. In late 2002, another decision was made to not incorporate smart card acceptance at on-street parking meters. These decisions resulted from a lack of funding for software development, as well as the delays that this additional

---

[18] The LYNX vehicles have two existing driver interfaces, for the farebox and the automated next stop announcement system.

software development would have required. Each of these decisions adversely affected the number of parking participants in the study.

- **Limited Scale of the FOT Test Configuration:** The implementing agencies took into account the cost and the time available for implementation when establishing the scale of the FOT test configuration (i.e., the routes and locations for which to include smart card accepting equipment). The implementing agencies also indicated that risk management was taken into account at certain decision points. One example was in considering the potential expense related to the escalating integration issues often prevalent when integrating with legacy systems using a limited budget. Another example was selecting payment applications that took existing patents (e.g., the process patent for the use of transponders to pay for parking) into account. In order to maximize the scale of the FOT test configuration (i.e., given the limited budget), private sector partners were sought who were motivated to volunteer their services and equipment (i.e., at reduced or no cost to the project).

The decision to avoid toll system integration was one factor that led to the selection of EFKON equipment. EFKON supplied the equipment necessary to equip the busiest toll plaza in the OOCEA system. The partnership agreed to include EFKON in its outreach efforts, detailing the services and equipment supplied during the project.

The quantity of equipment supplied by Ascom met the request from the ORANGES partners for outfitting the Link 101-bus route and the LASER (University of Central Florida circulator) route on the LYNX system. However, both routes were unexpectedly discontinued during the course of the project due to a loss of funding from outside agencies. Two other bus routes were selected (Links 13 & 15) in place of Link 101. This change limited where the smart card would be accepted and impacted the potential pool of cardholders. For example, LYNX pass users who typically use non-equipped routes would be less likely to be interested in the smart card (since a pass on the smart card would not be usable on these routes).

- **Duration of Implementation Period:** As was discussed earlier, the overall implementation period (from the start of development through to the ORANGES cards being used by actual cardholders in revenue service) took longer than the implementation team had originally planned. The original plan allocated 11 months to develop an integrated demonstration system in an office environment, followed by a 12-month period until the full test configuration for the revenue service demonstration system would be in place. This 12-month period was intended to be divided into stages. An initial limited scale FOT test configuration was supposed to be put in place over a 7-month period, followed by an expansion to the full-scale test configuration over the remaining 5 months of the rollout period. However, the overall development period increased from a planned 23 months to 28 months. This was due in part to increased time being required for the initial systems integration stage, which appears to have involved several factors:

- **Equipment Selection:** As discussed earlier, several complications arose and reassessments were required as the implementation team selected the appropriate smart card, readers and equipment retrofits for installation.

- **Vendor Agreements:** Agreements enabling use of the Ascom and EFKON equipment were not executed until June 2002, 14 months <u>after</u> the start of the FOT development.

- **Systems Integration across Modes/Additional Toll Component:** Decisions about the specific nature of the parking field equipment (and the addition of the laneside readers to the toll plaza component) were not resolved with suppliers until October 2002.

- **LYNX Service Changes:** In late 2002, an additional delay arose due to changes in LYNX's operational funding from outside sponsors; this resulted in cancellation of the routes that had been intended for use in the FOT. Alternative routes had to be selected that could use a similar number of the Ascom validators, since this quantity had already been agreed on.

- **Supplier Production Delays:** In July/August 2003, there were delays in receiving the smart card shipment. This delayed the initial enrollment of cardholders and card distribution, even though the cardholders had already been recruited.

- **Software/Systems Integration:** There were systems integration delays for a variety of reasons, including limits on the availability of TranSend staff resources. The decision to use some demonstration equipment provided by the vendors at no or reduced cost appears to have increased the complexity and time required for the integration effort. Although the vendors provided the equipment and in some cases support services and the associated software, they did not provide as much software customization and integration support services as would be typical in a non-FOT environment. This meant additional responsibility for the systems integrator, which exacerbated the system integration delays.

- **Deferred System Functionality:** The initial FOT test configuration in August 2003 did not include the EFKON smart card enabled transponder. The central clearinghouse system processed the various payments and revaluing transactions retrieved from field equipment to enable appropriate funds transfers among participant accounts, rather than maintaining centralized account balances. However, centralized account balances are needed for smart card accepting transponders. The systems integrator needed additional time to support this functionality, and the implementing agencies decided to launch the FOT without the smart card accepting transponders, rather than further delay the system launch. The smart card enabled transponder capability was finally brought into revenue service in January 2004.

- **Limited Card Activity:** The implementing agencies initially intended to issue 150-500 smart cards. This was considered by the federal evaluation team in its risk analysis to represent too low a number of cardholders to allow for useful results. There was also a concern that some issued cards might not remain in regular use throughout the demonstration period. As a result, the implementing agencies agreed that sufficient cards would be issued to achieve 800-1200 active cards throughout the 12-month evaluation period (i.e., issuing additional cards if some became inactive).

It was agreed that a card would be considered inactive if it had not been used at least once within three consecutive weeks. Although the agencies used a pre-screening method to select cardholders, with each agency offering an incentive (either to initially try out the card or on an ongoing basis), the level of cardholder transaction activity remained quite limited throughout the demonstration; there were never more than 160 active cardholders.

The initial group of cardholders was recruited in May-June 2003, and the initial version of the system became operational in August 2003. As a result of system integration and smart card delivery delays, cardholders did not receive their smart cards until the third week in August 2003. The delay between cardholder recruitment and card delivery appears to be one factor that had an adverse effect on participation.

Also, the recruitment of cardholders was not yet complete when the system became operational in August 2003. This resulted in part from the decision to defer recruiting 30-50 cardholders until the smart card accepting transponder functionality was operational in January 2004 (i.e., these cardholders also needed to be issued a smart card accepting transponder). Although 1000 cards had been issued by February 2004, and 1200 by May 2004, the number of active cards remained below 160 throughout the demonstration period.

A large proportion of those who received a card either never became active users or became inactive after some initial period of use. It appears that this low card use may well be related to the limited scale of the demonstration, since this inherently restricted the usefulness of the card, and required cardholders to also continue using conventional payment methods for other parts of their daily travel.

One approach to achieving the required number of active cards would have been for the agencies to issue a significantly greater number of cards. One problem preventing consideration of this approach was that, in September 2003, Gemplus informed the implementing agencies (with no prior warning) that the GemCombi dual interface smart card originally purchased had been discontinued and was no longer in production. The replacement dual interface card from Gemplus was to be based on the Java operating system and be "backwards compatible" with the existing readers. However, these cards were not expected to be available until 2005.

This obviously limited the ability of the agencies to order additional smart cards to supplement the original order.[19] However, although the original card order was for 2100 cards, the cumulative number of issued cards leading up to and during the demonstration did not exceed 1300. Thus, the low card usage seems to be partly associated with limitations in the ability to recruit the full planned complement of cardholders. This difficulty may have been related, as suggested above, to the limited scale of the demonstration, and thus the limited number of agency customers with an interest in using the card.

9.2 Lessons Learned

Key lessons learned from this FOT are as follows:

- **Institutional Collaboration**

  Diverse and multimodal transportation agencies can collaborate effectively on a regional smart card-based payment system: LYNX, OOCEA and the City of Orlando Parking Bureau have demonstrated that diverse and multimodal transportation agencies in a region can work together to establish an operational regional multimodal transportation smart card payment system using a third party clearinghouse service provider. To accomplish this, agency management needed to work through a variety of issues related to establishing roles/responsibilities and trust relationships.

  This success was accomplished through an ongoing commitment from top management to foster the success of the system, and frequent communications amongst a core management steering group. The ongoing commitment from top management was fostered through frequent briefings from the management steering group. In addition to other on-going communication mechanisms, monthly meetings were conducted for the purpose of coordinating the evaluation effort with the steering group.

---

[19] An option would have been to modify the system to accept a different card, but this would have had significant cost and time implications.

- ## Systems Integration

  ### A universal smart card and unified clearinghouse for multimodal regional transportation payments is feasible from a technical perspective: One of the key purposes of the FOT was to demonstrate the technical feasibility of implementing a universal smart card and a unified clearinghouse for multimodal regional transportation payments, where a card issued by any participating agency could be used for payments with (and revalued at) smart card equipment operated by any of the agencies.

  Previous regional smart card systems in the US have been primarily limited to supporting multiple transit agencies in a region (e.g., San Francisco TransLink), or to supporting the combination of transit and transit-related parking (e.g., Washington SmarTrip). The ORANGES FOT was successful in demonstrating that it is technically feasible to extend the underlying operational concept to encompass transit, tolls and parking. In addition, the toll usage successfully demonstrated the feasibility of smart card accepting transponders.

  ### It is important not to underestimate the complexity of integration and interoperability issues: The implementation team required considerably longer than originally planned to complete the system design and implementation. Most of the systems integration challenges centered around (1) determining the correct combination of smart card and readers, and (2) retrofitting the various types of existing field equipment. The primary factor further complicating these issues was that the vendors and suppliers were only willing to provide a limited amount of support (since they were not being paid). This issue could have been better addressed with documented requirements for the system prior to vendor selection.

  ### It is important to ensure that system testing checks for the proper handling of error conditions: Evaluation of the after testing results revealed an important error in how the overall system handled the case where a transaction amount exceeded the stored value balance (e.g., a $3 transaction when the balance was $1). Apparently, the card could not store a negative value and the result is a "roll under" condition with a very large positive number (approaching $43 million) recorded as the balance rather than the negative value.

  The card or card reader needs to include logic to prevent such a transaction from being completed. Barring that, the clearinghouse needs logic to detect/report such occurrences. None of this preventative or detection logic was in place in the FOT system. To detect this or a similar type of problem in future projects of this type, the system response to error conditions should be explicitly addressed through the testing and ongoing monitoring of the revenue service results.

- **Card Usage**

  Extra effort in initial cardholder recruitment, screening and education could pay dividends: The limited number of cards being issued made it essential that cardholders be properly screened as part of the recruitment process. The usage patterns of potential recruits were screened by agency customer service representatives and via the project website to attempt to recruit cardholders who used the actual routes and locations accepting the cards. Flyers were also handed out at the specific toll plaza and parking garages where the cards were to be accepted. LYNX recruiting was completed on-board buses and at bus stops (for Link 13 & Link 15) by a professional recruiting firm.

  Despite these efforts, some of the initially recruited cardholders only used their cards for a brief time, while others used them only sporadically. It is possible that some adjustments to the recruitment approach could have helped in identifying cardholders more likely to use the card. Insight into this might be gained through follow-up interviews with cardholders.

  It also appears that the agency capability for recruiting additional cardholders later in the trial was limited. Although a total of 2100 cards were available – and the number of cards in active use remained below 160 throughout the demonstration period – many of the cards were never issued. The initial recruitment drive led to about 750 cards being issued by mid-September 2003. Recruitment efforts were renewed beginning in November 2003, subsequent to the number of active cards dropping below 100. This led to a gradual and steady issuance of additional cards over the remainder of the trial, culminating in an overall cumulative total of 1250 cards issued by late June 2004 (after which no further cards were issued).

  In any case, additional education/outreach for cardholders at the outset and from time to time during the FOT might also have helped identify opportunities to increase cardholder use of the system.

  The limited scale of the FOT test configuration and limited staff training made the card less useful and attractive: The limited number of card acceptance locations seems to have been a disincentive toward extensive and continuous use. Comments from the after discussion groups indicated that factors that made card use less attractive included (1) the limited number of revaluing locations; (2) the fact that the card could not be used with all bus routes and toll plazas; and (3) limited agency staff awareness/training about accepting the card.

In particular, cardholders indicated that although they were users of the equipped routes and locations, they may have used the card more if a broader range of routes and locations had been equipped to accept the card. These cardholders also mentioned staff training issues (e.g., some LYNX drivers were reportedly not familiar with the fact that the smart card was an accepted fare medium or how it was used with the validator). Comments from the planning and management after discussion group indicated that the agencies recognized that a more comprehensive scale for the FOT test configuration and more extensive training would likely have improved the results.

- **Equipment Inventory and Suppliers**

  It is important to order more smart cards than the agencies initially think they will need: Smart card systems can switch to a new smart card from that originally selected, but only with additional costs to reconfigure the readers to accept the new cards. After the mandatory requirement for maintaining 800-1000 active cards throughout the 12-month demonstration period was established, the agencies attempted to order more smart cards from the supplier (Gemplus) to supplement the original order of 2100 cards. However, it turned out that this particular type of smart card had been discontinued. As Gemplus demonstrated here, card products can be discontinued before the replacement product is available – or conceivably without offering a replacement at all – and with little warning to current customers. In deciding how many cards to order initially, the implementation team had mistakenly assumed that they would be able to order additional cards if needed.

- **Developing Effective Equipment Procurement and Cost Control Strategies**

  There are tradeoffs with using reduced cost equipment in a demonstration project: The implementation team made arrangements with several vendors to supply equipment at a reduced price (or in some cases at no cost) in consideration of the relatively high profile that this involvement would provide. While vendors did agree to offer lower cost equipment, some offered only limited quantities. In addition, some software customization and systems integration support services that would typically be offered by an equipment vendor became the responsibility of the overall systems integrator.

  The implementing agencies indicated that this approach was based on a risk management decision that took into account the odds for success and cost estimates received for integration with existing systems. They estimated that half of the federal funding provided for the project might have been expended for this part of the overall integration effort if this approach had not been adopted. The implementation team identified these equipment arrangements with vendors as a viable implementation solution, given the available funding, once it was clear that initial attempts at a traditional procurement approach had proven unacceptable from a risk management perspective. The revised procurement approach that was utilized served to limit the need to use capital project funding for equipment purchases. The limited scale of the test configuration also helped preserve sufficient funding to last throughout the duration of the FOT.

- ## Cardholder Incentives

    Incentive schemes can affect results: The cardholder incentives established by the agencies apparently influenced usage patterns during the demonstration. OOCEA customers received a smart card with $5 preloaded, and were to receive a $20 check at the end of the 12-month trial if they have remained an active user throughout the FOT period. However, this incentive was discontinued after issuance of the initial 300 cards by OOCEA, as it was determined that many customers discontinued use of the smart card once the initial five dollars had been used. Transit and parking customers received a discount for each ORANGES transaction processed throughout the demonstration (15% for LYNX fares and 50% for parking fees). Parking was the most frequent type of ORANGES transaction, which raises the possibility that there might have been fewer ORANGES parking transactions if the incentive had not been as generous.

    Other types of incentives identified as being of interest (i.e., in the after cardholders discussion group) included: (1) incentives tied to higher revaluing amounts or card balances; (2) incentives tied to frequency of card use; (3) a loyalty program where points could accumulate for discounts with retailers or community activities; and (4) occasional random free payments when using the card.

- ## Evaluation Data Collection

    Larger data samples should be collected whenever possible: In some cases, the before and after data analysis found that the 95% confidence intervals for the before and after samples overlapped. This does not provide evidence to support a statistically significant change between the before and after periods. Larger sample sizes would likely have decreased the size of the confidence intervals, increasing the opportunities to reveal evidence of a statistically significant change.

    Delays in collecting data should be avoided: LYNX attempted to gather accumulated APC data from the equipped buses near the end of the after data collection period. Unfortunately, only at that point did LYNX become aware that door sensor malfunctions had prevented APC data collection throughout much of the after data collection period. If the data had been retrieved more frequently (e.g., weekly) the door sensor problems could have been identified and resolved quickly, providing much more data.

10 Conclusions and Recommendations for Future Regional Deployments of Multimodal Electronic Payment Systems

This report has presented the results of the USDOT evaluation of the ORANGES Electronic Payment Systems Field Operational Test. The evaluation included development of a comprehensive set of goals based on a consensus building process with the implementing agencies, as well as feasible and practical measures and data collection methods. These data collection methods were used to collect quantitative and qualitative before and after data. The before and after analysis has helped identify potential benefits from multimodal electronic payment systems.

Based on the issues and lessons learned from the ORANGES FOT demonstration, the following actions are recommended for agencies intending to deploy a similar multimodal system:

- **Deploy to Fully Meet Traveler Needs:** It appears that one factor limiting card usage in the ORANGES demonstration was that the limited scale of the test configuration did not fully meet traveler needs. LYNX cardholders still needed to use conventional paper transfers and period passes for trips involving non-equipped routes. OOCEA toll users still needed to use a conventional EPASS transponder or cash for non-equipped toll plazas along their travel route. On the other hand, card use at a parking garage addressed the entire payment need for that trip, which may help explain the higher observed usage levels for parking.

- **Foster Institutional Collaboration:** Agencies participating in the ORANGES demonstration established successful technical and interagency operations with a multimodal electronic payment system. This significant and groundbreaking achievement largely resulted from extensive and ongoing institutional collaboration efforts. Project champions took the initiative for ongoing outreach, which helped maintain support from senior management and foster the required new interagency working relationships.

- **Provide Extensive Training:** ORANGES discussion groups indicated that front-line staff involved with card acceptance and revaluing, as well as with customer service, need extensive and ongoing training to be able to operate the system effectively and maintain cardholder confidence.

- **Use Risk Analysis:** Risk analysis can help identify and address risks prior to deployment. The ORANGES demonstration risk analysis identified risks in advance from the limited number of intended cards and acceptance/revaluing locations. Although financial constraints prevented the agencies from increasing the number of acceptance/revaluing locations, the number of issued cards was increased. In the end, this served to help compensate for the low card usage.

- **Ensure Long Term Smart Card Supply:** After placing the initial order, the ORANGES agencies attempted to order additional smart cards but were informed that this card had been discontinued. This illustrates that the future supply of any particular smart card cannot be assured, so it is critical to select smart card readers that can read cards from multiple vendors (or be adapted to do so).

- **Plan on Development Time for Integration Issues with Legacy Equipment:** Parking needed to integrate the card readers with its existing equipment, and integration timing/funding challenges led to excluding parking kiosks and meters from the demonstration. For OOCEA, EFKON equipment – separate from the existing equipment -- was selected to minimize any impact on existing toll plaza systems. However, the smart card reader type supported by this toll equipment was not yet supported by the LYNX fareboxes; this led to LYNX using a stand-alone smart card reader. The point is that significant time was needed to identify and address the various compatibility issues involved with accepting a universal smart card type in the legacy equipment environment of multiple agencies.

- **Monitor System Data During Initial Operations:** Analysis of after data revealed that the system was not handling negative balances correctly. No part of the overall system had been configured with the necessary logic to complete such transactions correctly or to detect/report if such transactions were completed incorrectly. Although this issue was not detected during system acceptance testing, it could have been identified through ongoing periodic reviews of system data by the implementing agencies.

www.ingramcontent.com/pod-product-compliance
Lightning Source LLC
Chambersburg PA
CBHW081119290526
45795CB00006B/2182